D0908735

About the author

TOBY SHELLEY has reported from many countries in the Middle East, North Africa and sub-Saharan Africa over the course of twenty years as a journalist. He works for the *Financial Times*. Previously he was regional energy news editor for Dow Jones Newswires. His most recent book is *Oil: Politics, Poverty and the Planet* (Zed Books, 2005). He is a member of the council of management of the radical development charity War on Want.

Nanotechnology

New Promises, New Dangers

———————

Toby Shelley

Fernwood Publishing
Nova Scotia

Books for Change
Bangalore

SIRD
Kuala Lumpur

David Philip
Cape Town

ZED BOOKS
London & New York

Nanotechnology was first published in 2006 by

In Canada: Fernwood Publishing Ltd,
8422 St Margaret's Bay Road (Hwy 3) Site 2A, Box 5,
Black Point, Nova Scotia, B0J 1B0

In India: Books for Change,
139 Richmond Road, Bangalore 560 025

In Malaysia: Strategic Information Research Development (SIRD),
No. 11/4E, Petaling Jaya, 46200 Selangor

In Southern Africa: David Philip (an imprint of New Africa Books),
99 Garfield Road, Claremont 7700, South Africa

In the rest of the world: Zed Books Ltd, 7 Cynthia Street, London N1 9JF,
UK, and Room 400, 175 Fifth Avenue, New York, NY 10010, USA
www.zedbooks.co.uk

Designed and typeset in Monotype Bembo by illuminati, Grosmont
www.illuminatibooks.co.uk
Cover designed by Andrew Corbett
Printed and bound in Malta by Gutenberg Press

Distributed in the USA exclusively by Palgrave Macmillan, a division of
St Martin's Press, LLC, 175 Fifth Avenue, New York, NY 10010

A catalogue record for this book is available from the British Library
Library of Congress Cataloging-in-Publication Data available

Library and Archives Canada Cataloguing in Publication
Shelley, Toby
    Nanotechnology: new promises, new dangers / Toby Shelley.
    ISBN 1-55266-192-X
    1. Nanotechnology.   I. Title.
    T174.7.S54 2006   620´.5
    C2005–907270–9

        ISBN 983 2535 794 Pb (Malaysia)

        ISBN 1 84277 686 X Hb (Zed)
        ISBN 1 84277 687 8 Pb (Zed)
        ISBN 978 1 84277 686 5 Hb
        ISBN 978 1 84277 687 2 Pb

Contents

Introduction

The control of technology defines wealth and power. The control of new technologies shapes and reshapes wealth and power relations whether between countries or corporations.

From a description of an individual's or a community's access to technology – be it sanitation or information technology, transport or weaponry – we can generally derive a definition of social status, power and even geographic location. But access should not be conflated with exposure. Millions of workers churning out computer components in factories in Asia may never have access to a personal computer but are exposed to the social relations and health hazards the industry brings. Similarly, the civilian victims of high-technology arsenals endure exposure but scarcely have access to the breakthroughs made by scientists employed by the military.

The demand for control over the development and deployment of new technology is, then, a political demand. It challenges the right of governments and corporations to define the uses to which technology is put – swords or ploughshares – and to impose the costs of producing and consuming new products or employing new work processes, whether it be new forms of pollution or hazards at work or dangers on the supermarket shelves.

Nanotechnology deals with materials and processes at a scarcely conceivable smallness, measured in billionths of a metre. At that scale, familiar materials such as carbon may exhibit properties unfamiliar at a larger scale. Processes may be carried out with extraordinary precision. The exploitation of nanoscale properties, such as enormous strength, enhanced catalysis, reaction to light, electrical conductivity, has potential applications for just about every aspect of life from the medical to the military, manufacturing processes and demand for raw materials.

Indeed for some the range of applications envisaged for nano-technology has become so great they question whether the term is any more than a catch-all phrase used to attract funding for research. (Others have tried, unsuccessfully it seems, to keep the phrase to a narrow definition centred on manufacture using nanoscale tools.) Forecasts for the financial importance of nano-technology are impressive.

The promises made by some exponents of nanotechnology are at least as grandiose as those made by previous prophets and profiteers of new technologies. It will feed the world. It will cure cancer. It will enable pollution-free energy. Experience teaches us to suspect that behind these promises lie environmental degradation, reinforced global power relations and a yet greater chasm between the haves and the have-nots.

Yet the potential is vast for nanotechnology to be deployed in ways that bring massive benefits to the poor of the world as well as the wealthy consumers of the North and its outposts among the affluent of the South. The question is: who will decide where the research funding goes and what products and processes are sanctioned?

This book is intended to bring to the reader's attention some of the areas in which nanotechnology is being applied, to look at who is controlling the development of the new technology. It highlights the potential benefits that nanotechnology might deliver and also examines some of the dangers it may pose to consumers, producers, the environment, and the very way in which we view the world and ourselves.

It calls for civil society to seize upon the implications of nano-technology (and indeed other emerging technologies), to ensure access to its benefits, to police exposure to its disbenefits, and to make the political demand to control it.

I

The emerging world of nanotechnology

Tramways and buckyballs

Every week, specialist newsletters report bewildering new advances in nanoscale science in the laboratories of universities and institutions. In one wholly unexceptional week Massachusetts Institute of Technology reported that researchers had discovered how to keep alive for three weeks a protein found in spinach that captures the energy from sunlight, while it was in contact with electronic equipment. Meanwhile, at the University of Pittsburgh there was excitement as scientists said they could now produce perfectly uniform tubes with a diameter one-thousandth that of a human hair. Not only were the tubes uniform but with a simple process they would arrange themselves into a carpet-like formation and when exposed to acids or detergents would change colour.

In Boston University the department of physics announced it had fabricated tiny switches out of silicon that would open and shut millions of times per second using infinitesimally small amounts of electricity. A few days earlier a transatlantic team said it had made progress towards building a nanoscale tramway out of DNA – the substance that carries the code that determines the characteristics of living things. Using strands of DNA the scientists were able to move unimaginably small fragments of material from one place on a nanoscale structure to another along a predetermined route. At Rice University in the US in the same few days it was announced that researchers had found a way to reduce the toxicity of buckyballs, football-shaped constructs of 60 carbon atoms, by attaching other molecules to them.

In university laboratories all over the world more and more money and time are going into the creation and manipulation of these nanotubes and buckyballs and quantum dots (pieces of a material such as gold that at the nanoscale have different properties to those they have at a larger scale).

These advances sound abstruse to the layperson but for most researchers the days of science for science's sake are long gone. Their work is a bridge between theory and commercial application. Keeping the spinach protein alive without feeding it its usual fare of water and salt will interest computer and mobile phone manufacturers because photosynthesis, the chemical conversion of sunlight into energy, could be used to power electronic equipment – but not if the requisite proteins require salt and water, both of which are seriously inimical to electronics.

The self-assembling nanotube carpet has potential applications as a sensor, indicating the presence or absence of particular environmental conditions. But the researchers also discovered it had another quality, that of a biocide. The tiny tubes were found to spear and kill E. coli bacteria. That raises the possibility of creating surfaces, perhaps in hospitals or kitchens, that eliminate potentially dangerous bacteria.

Further news of Boston's ultra-fast silicon switch will be watched by computer memory manufacturers because the efficiency of computer chips is based around the size, density and speed of tiny on–off switches or gates. The Boston team's switches achieved a work rate of millions of cycles per second – many, many times the speed of current laptop computers.

The miniature tramway addresses one of the basic problems of nanotechnology: how to devise mechanisms that will place molecules just where they are wanted, enabling construction to be carried out automatically rather than individual piece by individual piece. It is part of the quest to turn construction at the nanoscale from a laborious, lab-based activity into a commercially viable assembly-line function.

Controlling the toxicity of buckyballs is significant from two points of view. First, because one proposed use for them has been to attack bacteria or cancerous cells, in which case their toxicity is useful as long as it is controlled. But, second, they might have far wider applications in material used, for instance, in fuel cells. As a major emerging concern over nanomaterials is their potential to harm people and the environment, for those pursuing commercial applications to be able to say toxicity can be switched off could prove crucially important.

It is those commercial applications that excite the research divisions of multinationals such as GE and Bayer and General Motors. GE Global Research announced in 2004 it had broken existing records in the manufacture of organic light-emitting diodes and could now make paper-thin sheets of light-emitting material of a size and brightness previously unattained. Bayer, the giant German chemicals and pharmaceuticals group, devoted an edition of its scientific magazine to nanotechnology and said all of its divisions were engaged in research with applications that ranged from impregnating leather with long-lasting fragrances to improving food packaging to designing dyes for use in diagnosing diseases. General Motors has begun introducing composites of nanomaterials in the bodywork of the Impala, a high-selling car.

Sandia, based in New Mexico, is a US government National Nuclear Security Administration laboratory. It has been exploring a phenomenon whereby minute disturbances to an arrangement of nanoscale 'combs' produce a much larger and easily measurable change in the amplitude of a light shone through it. This could lead to the production of small, highly sensitive sensors that could be used in navigation systems.

A small British company called Hydrogen Solar has developed a nanoscale material that it says doubles the performance of its technology for converting light and water into hydrogen for use as a fuel.

In Pune in India, the National Chemical Laboratory has built nanoscale 'Golden Triangles' comprising particles of gold and essence of lemongrass. These, it is hoped, can be used alongside cancer-hunting antibodies.

Whether in academic institutions, multinationals, start-up companies or defence establishments, the search is on and the funding is rising. Researchers all over the world are deployed on projects to build transistors made of a single molecule, molecular motors modelled on protein motors in the body, carbon nanotube wire and a host of other components measured in billionths of a metre.

Research matters to companies because technological leadership in a global economy leads to more and 'better' goods and services produced more cheaply, and that brings competitive advantage. For governments there is the allure of superiority in security, intelligence and trade.

To a greater or lesser extent, the commercialisation of research brings change to workers in affected industries and services and to consumers of goods and services. The key question is how great or small the impact of a given technology will be. Will it merely modify existing patterns of work and consumption? Will it signal the demise of household-name companies, replace them with new corporations, or give them new leases of life? Will whole industries be superseded? Does the new technology herald and enable massive industrial, social and geopolitical change?

A cursory look at the second half of the twentieth century and the first years of this century reveals a plethora of major changes to the world economy, the rise of new industrial powers from Japan to the Asian Tigers to China, facilitated in large part by the export of existing technologies and also jobs. New techniques changed agriculture in India and Indonesia through the so-called Green Revolution. Development of containerisation in the shipping industry made feasible the rapid transit needed for a global economy. Developments in the petrochemical industry introduced the plastics without which little of contemporary industry, from armaments to toys, packaging to computing, is imaginable.

Changes to employment patterns around the world are tumultuous. The member states of the Organisation for Economic Cooperation and Development were referred to as the industrialised world. Increasingly they are post-industrial, with growing dependence on factories and workers in the developing world, particularly China. There, 120 million farmers have migrated to the cities of Guangdong, Fujian and Zhejiang provinces since the end of the 1970s, leaving poor western and central agricultural areas bereft of young people. By 2020 the number will reach 210 million. Parts of India have carved out niches as centres of expertise in software development or as call-centre locations.

Yet all of these changes spring from the nexus of technological and social developments of the Industrial Revolution. In that era, defined by some as the period 1780 to 1880 but arguably stretching from the late seventeenth century at least through to Henry Ford's first volume car production, science married with capital and the two spawned an increasingly internationally rapacious social order that generated goods and profits from primary commodities and labour the world over.

Nanotechnology: a new age dawning?

For some, the cluster of new technologies of which nanotechnology is a major piece, but which also includes genetic engineering, cognitive science and information technology, are the modern-day equivalents of the breakthroughs in iron and steel making, steam-powered locomotion, textile manufacturing and so on that enabled the social and political transformation of the world that began two centuries ago and that continues to shape and reshape the economies of the world.

Eddie Bernice Johnson, a senior member of the US House of Representatives' science committee remarked:

> The ages of civilization are designated by reference to a prominent material that could be fashioned by the prevailing state of technology. For example, the Stone Age, the Bronze Age and the Iron Age. Now we are at the threshold of an age in which materials can be fashioned atom by atom.[1]

Eric Drexler, perhaps the first theoretician of nanotechnology (and one of two men with a claim to having coined the phrase) prophesied a world of 'replicating assemblers', nanoscale functionaries that 'Powered by fuels or sunlight will be able to make almost anything (including more of themselves) from common material'.[2] Famously, he envisages the 'growing' of a rocket engine inside a vat of fluids and replicators. Extrapolating from this he points out that 'Most people in most states … function either as workers, larval workers, or worker rearers, and most of these workers make, move or grow things. A state with replicating assemblers would not need such work.'[3]

A decade and a half later, Mark Gubrud wrote a paper for Drexler's Foresight Institute in which he raised the spectre (his term) of a reshaped global economy where molecular manufacturing – nanotechnology – would massively reduce the call on primary commodities, re-localise manufacturing, and where 'A world system based on wage labour, transnational capitalism and global markets will necessarily give way.'

In 2003, the US House of Representatives science committee heard testimony from inventor and entrepreneur Ray Kurzweil that a 'golden age' of nanotechnology: 'will bring us the ability to essentially convert software, i.e. information, directly into physical products. We will be able to produce virtually any product for pennies per pound.'[4]

The RAND Corporation was asked by the US National Intelligence Council to assess the potential of new technologies in the period to 2015. While taking a rather more sanguine view than the school of visionaries, its report concluded that the impact of the technologies examined could be large enough to 'create real economic disparities both between and within the developed and developing worlds'.[5] The ETC Group, an ecological institute that monitors technology, injects a note of scepticism, reminding that 'The hype surrounding nanoscale technologies today is eerily reminiscent of the early promises of biotech. This time we're told that nano will eradicate poverty by providing material goods (pollution free!) to all the world's people, cure disease, reverse global warming, extend life spans and solve the energy crisis.'[6]

So far, the excitement about nanotechnology within industry has been generated not by debate over its social and political implications or the potential some see in it to replace human labour and transform work processes. Rather, the websites of numerous companies, from niche start-ups to global corporations concentrate on the advances it may offer for their products through new ma-

terials rather than new processes. Mundanely, glass manufacturers
are excited by self-cleaning window panes, bathroom manufacturers
by sinks to which dirt cannot stick, clothes makers by dirt-resistant
textiles. On a somewhat more grandiose scale, the computer chip
industry looks to nanotechnology as an escape route from the
cul-de-sac implied by Moore's laws (of which more later).

The divergence between the prophets and the profiteers – a
notional dichotomy as prophets such as Drexler are themselves often
involved in would-be commercial companies – or the visionaries
and those who see themselves as realists came to a head in a clash
between Drexler and Nobel prizewinner Richard Smalley, the
scientist who discovered the buckyball. In an exchange in the
US magazine *Chemical and Engineering News*,[7] Smalley refuted the
possibility of molecular assemblers, accusing Drexler of living 'in
a pretend world where atoms go where you want because your
computer programme directs them to go there'. Scathingly, he
concluded:

> You and people around you have scared our children. I don't expect
> you to stop, but I hope others in the chemical community will
> join me in turning on the light, and showing our children that,
> while our future in the real world will be challenging and there
> are real risks, there will be no such monster as the self-replicating
> mechanical nanobot of your dreams.

Their exchange – in which Drexler strongly defended his position – went beyond the realms of theory. For his part, Smalley
formed Carbon Nanotechnologies, which aims to supply nanotubes
for a variety of industrial applications. For the visionaries, concentration on new nanoscale materials rather than processes strips
technology from the term 'nanotechnology', in the end reducing
the new science to a ragbag of increments to existing technologies.
Drexler's longtime collaborator Ralph Merkle meantime teamed

up with a software entrepreneur to establish Zyvex, a company attempting to put nanoscale manufacture into practice.

As an article in *Wired*[8] pointed out, the Smalley approach won out in a crucial arena. In the '21st Century Nanotechnology Research and Development Act', George W. Bush allocated no less than $3.7 billion to development of nanoscale science. For a long while when the legislation was being drawn up it had looked as if a large chunk of this money and focus would be allotted to molecular manufacturing processes – the Drexler agenda. In the end, none went in that direction. The *Wired* article argued that the would-be manufacturers' ambitions were crushed by two opposing forces. One was the companies behind the NanoBusiness Alliance, which 'wasn't interested in anything as starry-eyed or scary as self-replicating molecular assemblers; it wanted to sell newfangled products like nanotech suntan lotion, ski-wax and paint.' The other force was the White House Office of Science and Technology Policy, which did not want to encourage anything that might generate the sort of public fears that had grown up around nuclear power and genetically modified foods.

The feasibility of replicators or nanobots and factories in a box remains hypothetical for now. The same can be said for the more utopian and dystopian visions of a society without workers. Realisation of the first would require great leaps of science if nanobots are even conceivable on the basis of current knowledge. The second would require realisation of the first plus nascent forms of social organisation that would or could exploit such technology. That is to say, nanotechnology in the looser sense of the term, embracing new materials, in alliance with other forms of sub-micro science combining over a long period of time to provide the basis for transformation comparable to the Industrial Revolution, also presupposes changes in social relations, certainly a negation of anything akin to a labour theory of value. If human labour were replaced across swathes of industry by self-sufficient, reproducible (not necessarily reproducing) nanobots, how would we value the items produced?

Additionally, it further presupposes that scientific advances present commercially or even logistically viable opportunities. Drawing energy from hydrogen has been feasible since the early nineteenth century, and the first fuel cells were invented in the middle of that century. The hydrogen economy is touted as the successor to the hydrocarbon economy but its realisation is dogged by the lack of viability of large-scale hydrogen production without the use of the hydrocarbons it is intended to replace. (This is, as it happens, an area in which nanotechnology may help out.)

Nonetheless, even the staid commentary of the Royal Society and Royal Academy of Engineering's report commissioned by the British government shows that nanotechnology, minus a lot of the hype, is bringing with it opportunities and dangers that cross all aspects of life for those living in the global economy, from medical to military, housework to personal and collective liberties.[9]

The following sections will illustrate some of the areas where nanotechnology is being or is likely to be applied in the near future. They will also highlight some of the more distant ambitions of developers, the points where what is probably achievable begins to merge with the visions of the prophets, defeat of sickness and old age, energy without pollution, a cataclysmic arms race, social control far beyond Orwell's nightmares.

Defining nanotechnology

It is often remarked but nonetheless worth repeating that nanoscale materials have been in use for some time. Carbon black, employed to strengthen vehicle tyres for a century, is a nanoscale material. Photographic processes also exploit nanoscale properties. Looking back centuries, the colouring found in some medieval pottery and deliberately created for stained-glass windows derives from the properties of materials at the nanoscale. Similarly, the naturally occurring nanoscale particles found in some clays and rare earths have long been exploited by the construction industry.

What distinguishes nanoscience and nanotechnology from these earlier applications is an understanding that the materials act as they do because of properties they possess at the nanoscale but not at the micro- (millionths of a metre) or larger scales, and the systematic attempt to predict, control and exploit those properties. In other words, it is the transition from the accidental to the deliberate, meaning a researcher, an engineer, an investor can move from wishing she or he could produce a material that bonds as well as a mussel does to a rock or a gecko does to a ceiling, or repels water as a lotus leaf does, to understanding how it is done and how to replicate it. That replication might involve any or a mixture of nanoscale materials, processes or tools.

This is the loose definition that will be used in this book and it is one that is increasingly current. However, it is not uncontroversial. To all intents and purposes it accepts the defeat of the Drexler definition, which draws on the visionary founding document of nanotechnology, a 1959 talk by Nobel prizewinner Richard Feynman.[10] For Drexler, Feynman's vision 'projects the development of nanomachines able to build nanomachines and other products with atom-by-atom control'.[11] Something akin to this definition permeated US government thinking through President Clinton's launch of the National Nanotechnology Institute, he argues. Since then, the term has been appropriated and distorted as business interests have misunderstood the concept, sought to benefit from the prestige (and funding) it attracted, and disposed of the awkwardly long-term nature of its promise and the dangers of the fears it generated. So Drexler wrote:

Dr Samuel I. Stupp of Northwestern University gave as examples of nanotechnologies 'pigments in paints; cutting tools and wear resistant coatings; pharmaceuticals and drugs; nanoscale particles and thin films in electronic devices; jewelry, optical and semiconductor wafer polishing'. Any connection between this miscellany of technologies and a research program inspired by the Feynman vision is almost imperceptible.[12]

The question of definition is not merely semantic. Forging and maintaining a widely accepted definition of nanotechnology has important implications for its commercialisation. Although there were moves afoot, at the time of writing there was no overarching nanotechnology classification in the world's most important patent offices. There is also no nanotechnology category in business classifications such as that used by the FTSE indices. This is important because it suggests there is not, yet at any rate, an identifiable nanotechnology industry or sector but rather a swathe of applications and potential applications spanning many other industries and sectors.

There are some indications that the applications of nanoscience have coherence, most notably perhaps the very fact that the terms 'nanoscience' and 'nanotechnology' are in currency and that there has been (and is) a battle over their employment. More concrete is the fact that the financial community is trying to define and then track the sector – Merrill Lynch has a 'Nanotech Index' of twenty-five companies involved in semiconductors, instrumentation, sensors, diagnostics and a range of other activities, and the future profits of each are deemed dependent on nanotechnology. Another sign is the emergence of geographic 'clusters' of expertise, possible precursors of a twenty-first-century Silicon Valley.

But Drexler's outrage at the 'miscellany of technologies' that are corralled into the nanotechnology pen does highlight the question whether the vulgar use of the term categorises a species or disguises a menagerie. As one industry analyst put it, those engineers who now find they need to know something about working at the nano-level still 'will think of themselves first as being in the defense, chemical, automotive or electronics industry – not the nanotechnology industry'.[13] He goes on to argue that an identifiable nanotechnology industry will emerge with a similar structure to the semiconductor industry, serving a host of sectors with very different requirements but with the bulk of business centred on a handful. In fact, the same analyst moves towards Drexler, identifying the 'glue' that holds the disparate applications together as comprising a clutch of processes used to build at the nano-level.

These processes are often divided into the top-down and bottom-up, depending on whether they involve shaving something down to the nanoscale or constructing a nanoscale item atom by atom. Self-assembly, molecular synthesis and the painfully slow atom-by-atom construction possible with scanning probe microscopes all fall into the latter category, while lithographic techniques fall into the former, hewing components out of chunks of raw material. Feynman mused about building a series of lathes where each was designed to replicate its predecessor in miniature, and even considered the conceptual difficulties the project would present.

On your high street now

The first fruits of deliberately applied nanoscience have been on the shop shelves for some time now, and the introduction of new commercial applications is likely to accelerate greatly. Indeed, it is the undebated introduction of nanomaterials into consumer products that has caused the most widespread concern about lack of regulation, to date. The campaign to label foods that has been genetically modified or contains genetically modified ingredients was vociferous and soon reached the highest echelons of trade diplomacy. The same has not happened – so far – with nano-materials.

In 2004, the ETC website reproduced an unofficial US Environmental Protection Agency document of some eight pages, listing current or very soon to be current commercial applications of nanomaterial by company, product name and function. These ranged from treatments for fabrics to laboratory equipment, sports equipment to lightweight armour, inkjet paper to drug delivery.

In their study cited above, the Royal Society and Royal Academy of Engineering listed a number of applications of nanomaterials that already touch the lives of consumers in richer economies, or were expected to do so within five years. These include:

1. Sunscreens and cosmetics. Titanium dioxide and zinc oxide at the nanoscale are transparent to visible light yet absorb or reflect the ultraviolet light that damages the skin of sunbathers. These two qualities enable manufacturers such as Johnson & Johnson and L'Oréal to manufacture 'invisible' sunscreen and anti-wrinkle cosmetics to pander further to consumer vanities. Iron oxide at the nanoscale is used for some lipsticks as a pigment.

2. Fabrics used for clothes, mattresses, upholstery and soft toys are increasingly treated with nanoscale coatings. Ability to control porosity at the nanoscale means the fabrics can be made water- or stain- or perspiration-resistant while retaining breathability. Household name brands such as Nike, Dockers, Savane, DKNY, Benetton and Levi's employ the new materials in some products, as do bedding makers Sleepmaker and Dreamland. A UK chemicals manufacturer and Woolmark created a joint

venture called Sensory Perception Technology with the selling 'proposition' that:

> Living in a world where vision is the dominant sense we often neglect our other senses, like touch and smell. But, imagine a sense-enriched world where your sportswear cools you on the move. Your shirt shrugs off the smell of tobacco or repels mosquitoes. You sink into fields-of-flowers on your sofa, catch the smell of success in a boardroom or hit a 'cool' note in a chic hotel lobby.

German chemicals giant Bayer has developed a technique for spraying leather and fabrics with microscopic droplets of perfume encapsulated in bubbles with a surface just nanometers in thickness. These penetrate the material and then release the perfume when pressure is applied.

3. Glazing and bathroom manufacturers are marketing self-cleaning windows and self-cleaning suites. Titanium dioxide at the nanoscale is again important to the self-cleaning applications as it can be engineered to repel water and be anti-bacterial. UK glass manufacturer Pilkington claims its product was the first of its kind on the market but St Gobain, for example, also has products available.

4. Nanocrystalline tungsten carbide, tantalum carbide and titanium carbide cutting tools have already found application in specialist areas such as boring holes in circuitboards.

5 Paint producers are likely to be major near-term users of nanomaterials and one interesting application began trials in Europe in 2004 with European Union funding. Millennium Chemicals developed a paint that uses the same ability of nanoscale titanium dioxide to absorb ultraviolet light that is exploited in sunscreens, in order to harness enough energy to convert nitrogen oxide pollutants in the air into nitric acid, which is naturally washed away or converted. The idea is that

the paint will neutralise some vehicle emissions. Anti-grafitti and crack-resistant paints using nanomaterials have been available for some time.

6. In 2002, General Motors, the world's biggest car maker, first introduced a nanocomposite material into the bodywork of a commercially sold vehicle. It is a clay with useful nanoscale properties dispersed within a plastic resin to form a relatively cheap material that saves weight (and so fuel) while being strong and, the company says, recyclable. Two years later it was introduced into the Impala, GM's highest volume car. At 540,000 lb a year, GM was the biggest user of such nanocomposites in the world.

7. Since the late 1960s the enhanced catalysing properties of some substances at the nanoscale – a result of the greater relative surface area of smaller particles – has been used in the oil refining and petrochemical industries to improve the yield of desired derivatives. Porous crystalline solids known as zeolites are particularly suitable. The efficiencies derived from using zeolites in oil refining were estimated in 1998 to save the US between $8 billion and $16 billion a year in oil imports.[14]

8. The information technology sector is one where nanotechnology is billed to have the biggest impact, as will become clear later. Already, the production of computer components has reached into the nanosphere as manufacturers seek to pack more and more processing power and memory into smaller and smaller spaces. In 2003, IBM introduced a new generation of personal computer hard drives that use a sandwich of materials a few atoms thick and with special magnetic properties allowing data storage capacity to be quadrupled. In 2004 computer chips had structures with widths of 130 nanometres – just above the common 100 nanometre definition of nanoscale – but were soon to reduce to 90 nanometres as new lithographic processes and

techniques came into play. Indeed, in August 2004, as Advanced Micro Devices said it had begun shipping microprocessors made using 90 nanometre technology, Taiwan's UMC and TSMC had already begun talking to customers about mass-producing chips using 65 nanometre technology in 2006.

9. Nanoparticles of calcium phosphate and protein are in use as a more effective way of blocking off tiny channels in the tooth that cause pain from cold food. The artificial apatite behaves just like natural tooth enamel.

An industry publication in December 2004 listed its top ten available nanotech products of the year. The majority, it found, had been commercialised through sports. The list of banal products ranged from footwarmers to washable mattresses, self-correcting golf balls to dental adhesive.[15]

The production of nanomaterials and related tools has itself already become a sizeable industry. ETC Group cited estimates in 2003 that 140 companies worldwide were producing nanoparticles such as buckyballs.[16] A German bank estimated that the market would reach $900 million in 2005.[17]

As manufacturing techniques have improved and production has been scaled up, the cost of making carbon nanotubes and buckyballs, regarded as basic building blocks of nanoscience, has fallen. In 1999, the cost of buckyballs was $600 a gram. Three years later it was $30.[18] In late 2004, Cyprus-based Rosseter Holdings was advertising nanotubes at $20–25 a gram and had the capacity to produce at least 30 grams per hour.[19] In the US, Richard Smalley's company Carbon Nanotubes expected to have a production capacity of 1,000 lb a day by 2005.[20]

In early 2003 fifty-five companies were making carbon nanotubes and at least twenty planning to sell industrial quantities – hundreds of tonnes – of buckyballs.

Taking a broad definition, sales of all nanotechnology-related products were calculated to have reached $54 billion as early as 2002.[21]

Limitless possibilities

The range of potential applications of nanoscale properties and materials is limitless and this is one of the grounds for claiming that moves by academia, government and commerce into the nano world herald a transformation of our lives. Here some potential short-, medium- and longer-term ambitions and aspirations are outlined for three crucial areas: energy, medicine, computing. In each case, the breadth of the industry, the plethora of research avenues and the rate at which developments are reported, mean that only an outline of some of the avenues is given. The issue of development and exploitation of nanomaterials, properties and technologies by the military and security apparatus is dealt with separately.

Energy

The efficiency of zeolites in oil refining and petrochemical production has already been referred to, but nanotechnology offers various approaches to energy production and consumption. Which ones are pursued and, if feasible, adopted is just as much a question of politics and price as of scientific success. As the RAND report noted:

> If the ready availability of oil continues, it may be difficult for technology trends to be much of a driving force in global energy between now and 2015. Key questions have to do with continued oil imports, continued use of coal, sources of natural gas, and the fate of nuclear power…

Significant changes in developed countries [however] may be driven more by existing social, political, and business forces, since the fuel mix of 2015 will still be strongly based on fossil fuels. Environmental concerns such as global warming and pollution might shift this direction, but it would likely require long-term economic problems (e.g. a prolonged rise in the price of oil) or distribution problems (e.g. supplies interrupted by military conflicts) to drive advances in renewable energy development.[22]

This analysis echoes that of the International Energy Agency, energy security watchdog of the rich countries of the Organisation of Economic Cooperation and Development, which has pointed out that it tends to be sharp oil price rises rather than treaties and manifestoes that spur energy efficiency drives.

Stephen Gillett (on whose 'White Paper'[23] on nanotechnology and energy some of the following paragraphs draw) also puts technological development within a politico-economic framework, labouring his concern about US dependence on foreign oil and ore. Nanotechnology has applications that can enable more efficient extraction and use of fossil fuels, applications that, used in isolation, would, of course, extend dependence on such fuels despite their overwhelming contribution to global warming. Gillett sees nanotechnology contributing to increased rates of recovery from reservoirs through advanced sensors. The super strength of some materials at the nanoscale offers the possibility of drills that can access deeper reserves.

Although the hydrocarbons most widely used are oil and natural gas, there are vast reserves of oil sand and bituminous crude in parts of the world such as Canada and Venezuela that can be processed into usable fuels but only at a cost that makes the commerciality of the operation viable relative to the price of conventional oil.

Some 40 per cent of the oil output of the Canadian province of Alberta in 2002 was from oil sands, equivalent to a third of national output and forecast to rise rapidly to 50 per cent. But some 2 tonnes of oil sands must be dug up to produce one barrel of oil. Even with oil prices at decade highs, in early 2004 cost overruns were causing concerns over some projects. Bioprocessing through the use of strains of enzyme derived from bacteria to break tar and asphalt reserves in the ground into useful products has long been mooted as a means of processing oil sands while reducing the need for environmentally damaging mining.

Interest is growing in gas hydrates, a frozen mixture of water, natural gas, mud and sand that occurs where conventional oil and natural gas do not – such as Japan, which is entirely dependent on imports. There are a number of ways in which the natural gas can be freed from the hydrate solid and Japan envisages production in 2012–16. Again, one of the options is bioprocessing. Potential reserves of natural gas in hydrates worldwide could exceed all reserves of all other fossil fuels, although this is meaningless unless they can be accessed at the right price.

Moving downstream, nanotechnology offers opportunities to reduce hydrocarbon consumption (or its growth, at least). The fuel efficiency of vehicles is directly correlated to their weight. As use of lightweight nanocompounds increases from the 7 per cent weight saving on side mouldings achieved by General Motors, towards some enthusiasts' ambition of a car that weighs less than its driver, so mileage per gallon will increase. Aircraft and ships will also see improvements. Other potential ways of improving hydrocarbon efficiency include nanoparticulate fuel additives and engine lubricants.

Widespread temperature and light management is certainly feasible through development of 'smart windows' that regulate use of other heating and cooling mechanisms according to the strength of prevailing sunshine. The amount of heat and light they allow to pass through them can also be regulated by manipulating the reactivity of the glass, rather like the way modern photochromic sunglasses adapt to light conditions.

Similarly, advances in LEDs (light-emitting diodes), which have a power requirement half that of conventional light bulbs, and LCDs (liquid crystal displays) will utilise nanotechnology. Current light bulbs are notoriously inefficient, wasting much of the energy they use through the emission of heat. The development of low-energy-intensity lighting panels, probably sensitive to the amount of available natural light, is just around the corner.

But does nanotechnology offer ways of breaking away from hydrocarbon (or wider fossil fuel) dependence? Fuel cells are presented as a means of shifting away from oil and gas and coal, with hydrogen seen as the most likely input. They escape what Gillett calls the Promethean Paradigm whereby fuels are burned, and operate under a paradigm more similar to that of the natural world where fuel is chemically converted into energy virtually without the gross inefficiency of loss as heat.

One of the conundrums of the hydrogen fuel cell is the sourcing of hydrogen. Most hydrogen is derived from hydrocarbons because of the current inefficiency of the alternative route – electrolysis. If nanotechnology can improve the efficiency of electrolysis, it contributes to a shift towards a hydrogen economy that is not underlain by indirect reliance on fossil fuels. The most likely way for it to do this is by improving the efficiency and availability of solar power generation to facilitate electrolysis.

Gillett identifies a number of other ways in which nanotechnology might benefit fuel cell development and a consequent shift away from large-scale thermal generation of power and towards power generated chemically at the level of the individual consumer or, by replacing batteries as well as power lines with fuel cells, the individual appliance. He identifies two particular areas where nanotechnology promises to help: improved catalysts – the materials that chivvy fuel molecules in a fuel cell into work; and better electrolytes – the material that contains and transports ions, allowing electrolysis to take place.

Ideally, catalysts should be tolerant of common contaminants such as carbon dioxide, should work at room temperature, operate with carbon-containing fuels (which need not be oil, gas or coal), and be considerably cheaper than at present. Electrolytes are better if they are solids rather than high-temperature, corrosive liquids.

At present, most fuel cells employ platinum group metals as catalysts. These are expensive and corrupt easily unless operated at high temperatures. Also, catalyst production has been an art rather than a science up to now. Nanotechnology should enable better engineering of existing catalysts to make them more efficient. Further ahead, Gillett hopes nanotechnology will enable new catalysts to be engineered that are less 'picky' about the reactants they work on, allowing use of alcohol fuels rather than difficult-to-handle hydrogen.

The search is on to find new solid electrolytes. Meanwhile, better control at the nanoscale of production of the electrolyte Nafion, used in commercial fuel cell units, could considerably improve its efficiency and price.

According to a European Commission research paper, 'Nano-technology will make solar energy a viable and lucrative proposition. Connective semiconductors of indium, gallium and nitrogen have already demonstrated performance figures that make solar cells with an efficiency level of 50 per cent seem feasible.'[24] Products using organic solar cells printed onto plastic film were expected on the market in 2005 with initial use on mobile phones and navigation equipment. Manufacturer Siemens expected efficiency to be doubled in the medium term.[25] A promising development reported from the University of Toronto in late 2004 was of particles of semiconductor crystals that can be tuned in to infrared light, meaning they could function from energy drawn from a light spectrum untapped by previous solar cells. Around half of the sun's energy is in the infrared spectrum and has not been tapped at all by previous solar panels. The crystal particles developed were so small they could be distributed in solvents, leading to the hope of rapid development of a sprayable infrared detector with a photovoltaic efficiency of 30 per cent. This is a step nearer to making solar energy gathering a function of any surface, from the walls of buildings to clothing to vehicles. Imagining the options for using a sprayable energy-gathering system, from self-refuelling vehicles to clothes generating energy to run computing and communications equipment or buildings that harvest power for themselves, one can easily imagine this being the 'killer application' that moves nanotechnology from promise to delivery.

The Graetzel cell is already in such mundane use as lighting Swiss watches. A dye molecule captures the energy from sunlight and shifts into a higher state, separating the charge and passing the electron from the dye molecule to a nanoparticle of titanium dioxide. The positive and negative charges are then allowed to recombine releasing energy at an efficiency of 7 per cent.[26]

Another contribution could be improving the storage of hydrogen in vehicles. Being a gas, hydrogen is less efficient at storing energy than is a liquid fuel such as petrol. But UK university researchers have discovered a way of injecting hydrogen atoms at high pressure into nanoscale pores of a material, where they are stored at much lower pressure for release later. A 'full tank' could provide fuel for 8,000 kilometres, according to some reports.

Medical

Medical diagnosis is already beginning to benefit from the properties that materials display at the nanoscale. Major advances in targeted treatment of illnesses and injuries, from cancers to eye infections to broken limbs, should follow.

Doctors have for some time used dyes to tag viruses and bacteria they want to identify or monitor. The idea is simple. Antibodies that will latch on to the target cell are marked with a dye that will show up or fluoresce under light of a particular wavelength. The amount of fluorescence can then be measured to ascertain the degree of infection. One problem is that the organic dyes that have worked can also be toxic. They also fade rapidly. Further, it is difficult to use different dyes at the same time because the emission light of one dye can be the same as the stimulating light of another, causing confusion in reading results. So, these dyes have been replaced by proteins that naturally fluoresce, but only if exposed to the right frequency of light. As different proteins and dyes absorb different frequencies, multiple light sources might be needed for multiple samples. The way round this is to employ nontoxic, nanoscale tags that are tiny enough to penetrate cell walls. Because of the nanoscale effect that colour depends on size, the tags can be engineered to different sizes, each size having a different target and fluorescing a different colour but all being stimulated by the same wavelength.

So far, much of the work in this area has been centred on quantum dots – semiconductor nanoparticles that can be manufactured. But some researchers – those at German pharmaceuticals company Bayer, for example – are following another route.[27] Quantum dots are expensive to make and often contain heavy metals. Nanophosphors are chemical compounds made up of silicates, oxides, sulphates or phosphates. They have the durability and multipurpose advantages of quantum dots but can be manufactured more readily and cheaply. This is because the light they emit does not depend on a carefully engineered size but on the type of ion embedded in them from a variety of rare earths, which are less environmentally damaging than heavy metals. Nanophosphors also fluoresce for a relatively long time, allowing the diagnostician to strip out background fluorescence that can cloud results. The next stage of development of nanophosphors is to find a way to couple reliably the inorganic tags to organic DNA segments that will seek out targets in the blood or saliva.

This high science is currently carried out in sophisticated research laboratories and possible early users include Nasa, the US space agency, which wants to monitor space radiation in astronauts. But practitioners also have in mind very small-scale, simple to use diagnostic kits that could be used relatively easily in the field to diagnose for a range of illnesses or carry out DNA testing. Imagine a handheld lab that could scan a sample of blood or saliva for a massive range of illnesses and conditions. Paul Alivisatos, a founder of the Quantum Dot Corporation, envisages a minute latex bead filled with a combination of quantum dots. When this is illuminated and the fluorescence is put through a prism, the result would be a 'spectral bar code' that could be compared to known sequences to find out which genes were active in which cells.[28]

Observation at the level of the single cell would allow for very early diagnosis and medication. A team at Harvard University in late 2004 was working on a prototype detector comprising an antibody that would latch on to a given virus particle, attached to a silicon nanowire transistor. When the antibody latched on to its target virus, the electrical conductance of the transistor changed. Conceptually, this opens the way to tiny devices carrying antibodies for thousands of viruses across which a patient's sample would be flowed, allowing the presence of any of the viruses to be detected.

A Canadian company has developed a sensor capable of identifying just five or ten bacteria in a liquid sample, allowing the very early detection of infection of individuals or indeed of environmental samples. Meanwhile, Rice University in the US has generated research showing that nanoparticles known as nanoshells, comprising a core of glass with a metallic coating, can enhance chemical sensing as much as 10 billion times because they are massively efficient at identifying substances through Raman scattering. That is the process by which molecules betray their identity by the way they reflect light. Nanoshells magnify the effect so that a disease protein or a toxin could be identified from just a few molecules.

Nanoscience may also provide breakthroughs in drug delivery, gene therapy and other forms of treatment. The Royal Society report lists a number of therapies under development where nanoparticle carriers transport drugs to target cells rather than just releasing them randomly into the bloodstream. 'Gene therapy, where the DNA has been packaged into a nanometre-scale particle, holds much promise for the treatment of genetic defects such as cystic fibrosis and immune deficiencies.'[29]

The large surface area of nanoparticles makes them particularly suitable for the role of mules in the body. Roukes mentions dendrimers – nanoscale molecules – as a promising example of a nanostructure that can be controlled. Perhaps they could be designed to swell and release a drug only when they are triggered by the presence of their target, so the drug would go right to and only to the infected area. Hollow nanoscale capsules are also being researched, as are glass and gold nanoshells that would release a drug when warmed. In late 2004 results were awaited of a silicon delivery system trial involving liver cancer patients in Singapore. The University of Texas found a nanoparticle formulation of a gene to significantly suppress lung tumour growth in rats.

That said, the Royal Society report downplays claims coming out of the US National Nanotechnology Institute that early and effective treatment of cancer tumours in their first year is conceivable by 2015, saying it demonstrated an 'oversimplistic view'.

The National Chemical Laboratory in India is one of the places where another approach was being trialled in 2004. Lemongrass extract added to gold ions in solution forms nanoscale triangles that can be attached to antibodies that guide them to cancer cells. The patient is then exposed to infrared light that does not affect normal body cells but heats up the triangles enough to cauterise the cancerous cells.

In Singapore, scientists have invented a contact lens made of a polymer to which drugs are added. These are then released in precise quantities directly to the eye, allowing the treatment of glaucoma. Research is also being carried out into artificial retinas.

Another area where nanoscience can contribute to medicine is in the repair and replacement of bone, where nanomaterials promise greater strength at lighter weight for prosthetics.

At the nanoscale, silver has antibacterial properties that are already being exploited for wound treatments. Unsurprisingly, the military is researching combat gear capable of locating and providing first aid to wounds.

In November 2004, Starpharma said it was ready to begin human trials with a vaginal microbiocide based on dendrimers to prevent transmission of HIV. The company claimed this was the first time a dendrimer-based drug had progressed from clinical to full human trials.

Information technology

The information and communications technology sector has been the primary driver for nanoscience. As the Royal Society report notes: 'the research into all aspects of semiconductor device fabrication, from fundamental physics to process technology, has dominated the nanoscience landscape and will continue to do so'.[30]

As with the energy sector, an understanding of and an ability to manipulate materials at the nanoscale presents the opportunity for both non-disruptive, incremental advances in current technologies and the grounds to aspire to new, wholly different ways of doing things.

In the energy sector the impetus for advance is threefold: the (declining) economic shock occasioned by periodic rises in oil prices; increasing costs of global warming; and competition between producers.

In the IT sector, a yardstick for measuring the performance of companies and the sector has been the rate of miniaturisation of computer components. The smaller the components, the more can be fitted into a given space, and the more that can be fitted, the more powerful the computer. As computers have become smaller and more powerful so they have become components of more and more consumers items. Computer chips control fridges, hi-fi equipment, wristwatches, cars and a myriad of other goods in the rich, consumer societies. This has been made possible by falling costs of production of the transistor, the tiny switch that is the building block of computing. In 1971 it cost 10 US cents to produce one, but by 2004 the cost was 0.001 cents.[31]

The rate of growth was sketched with remarkable accuracy and foresight by Gordon Moore, a founder of the Intel Corporation, in 1965. Moore's first law stated that the amount of space required for a transistor on a chip halves every eighteen months. In the early 1970s, the number of transistors per processor was little over 2,000. By the turn of the millennium it reached over 40 million. By 2007 it is forecast to hit 1 billion.

However, two major problems loom for the industry. The first is Moore's second and lesser known law, which holds that the cost of building a plant to manufacture chips doubles every thirty-six months. As two commentators note: 'Eventually the drive to downscale will run into extreme facility costs, and the market will reach equilibrium. Many experts project that this will happen around or before 2015, when a fabrication facility is projected to cost nearly $200 billion.'[32]

The second problem is that as the size of transistors falls and their number on a chip increases, so they will begin to rub up against constraints imposed by physics. As noted earlier, the tooling scales at which the industry operates is already at the nanoscale. The Ratners refer to the industry hitting a 'brick wall': when 'the transistor gets too small, quantum mechanical leaking of the electron through the transistor will mean that it is no longer clear whether the transistor is supposed to be on or off.'[33] As the wiring within chips shrinks to the nanoscale, the problem will be that the minute flow of electricity will wash away the wiring that is supposed to carry it.

Nanotechnology research is engaged in addressing these problems at several levels: that of the basic building block, the transistor; that of interconnection, the wiring; and that of the overall architecture of the system.[34]

In the laboratory, researchers are now able to coax molecules into acting as switches. The US corporation Hewlett Packard, as far back as 2002, said it had created a demonstration circuit with a 64-bit memory using molecules as switches. The device was so tiny that a thousand of them would fit on the end of a strand of hair.[35] Two years later, GE said it had constructed from a single nanotube a diode that could function as a transistor.

Initially, the efficiency of many devices put together in research laboratories is lower than that of established technologies, or the conditions under which they operate are more rigorous. But the limitations tumble away all the time. For example, one problem with nanotube transistors was that they would only work at very low temperatures. That limitation has now gone.

The nanotube is also a candidate to replace conventional wiring inside computer chips. But a further step is to use advances in building grids of nanotube wires. Using the ability of nanotubes to act both as wires and as transistors opens the way for them to be assembled into mechanisms in which they are both component and interconnection. Advances in controlling the growth of nano-tubes on the wafers on which chips are installed is opening the way to building 3D chips. By late 2004, the record length of a nanotube grown was 4 cm.

That said, the problems that remain with nanotubes are major. Consistent manufacture of nanotubes with the desired qualities has yet to be cracked and costs remain relatively high. Silicon nanowires represent an incremental change from current tech-nology but some developers consider them more dependable.

One of the defined targets of the computer industry is 'ambient intelligence', the integration of sensing, computing and com-munication into everyday objects at far lower costs than could be achieved using silicon as the building block. Polymer-based electronics may provide the cheap and flexible material while not requiring a shift away from established circuit and design tech-nology. Scientists in California have combined polystyrene with nanoscale gold particles to form high-density data storage material that can, potentially, be sprayed or painted into place.

Electrons display a characteristic known as 'spin', which reacts to magnetic conditions. This is already exploited in recent gen-eration hard disks, but research aims at taking it much further to produce computers that would not have to 'boot up' but could be switched straight on like a television. The principle at work is that rather than storing 'bits' of information in the form of a current that is either on or off, the data would be stored as a magnetic polarization or 'spin'. The advantages are that the data is held even when the current is turned off – hence the ability to restart instantly. Also, much larger amounts of data can be held in the same space as a conventional chip and only tiny electrical currents are required to change the polarization.

Problems that have faced researchers in this area include the temperatures at which nanoscale materials with the requisite qualities will operate. But progress is regularly reported, perhaps most promisingly in materials that can be blended with silicon, the material on which current chips are built, without changing the structure of the silicon. Nantero, a company trying to commercialise its Nonvolatile RAM technology, also argues that nanotube-based memory is highly resistant to heat, cold and magnetism.

Looking further ahead – certainly beyond 2015, according the RAND study – better understanding and control of materials at the nanoscale could bring about entirely new ways of computing. One of these is quantum switch computing, which would harness characteristics of electrons. Whereas contemporary computing is based on the on–off or 0–1 value of a 'bit' of information, quantum computing uses qubits that can be on and off, 0 and 1, at the same time. It is calculated that a 64-qubit device would be 18 billion trillion times more powerful than a modern 64-bit computer.[36]

Another paradigmatic technology would shift computing towards the realm of chemistry and biology rather than physics and electronics by using bio-molecular particles as switches operated by chemical rather than electrical stimuli.

The work for which such technology would be best suited is not the work done in most computer applications today. The most promising area for quantum switch computing is cryptography, where the ability to carry out a massive number of calculations in parallel is paramount. Here, quantum switch computing could reduce to a matter of minutes work that would otherwise take years. That leads to the spectre of secure transactions between customers and banks suddenly becoming insecure, so work is in progress on a cryptographic key comprising single photons transmitted over fibre-optic cables. The point is that any attempt to tap into the transmission would disrupt the photon flow, rendering the key useless.

Bio-molecular computing also offers massive parallel computing power, even at the experimental level capable of vastly outperforming large-scale supercomputers. And the electrical input is measured in billionths of a watt, meaning that the problem of overheating is avoided. Indeed, the working of the bio-molecular computer is essentially chemical, employing DNA, the nucleic acid that programmes life. DNA is capable of storing enormous amounts of information very efficiently in the form of a very limited number of possible combinations of molecules. The natural processes by which DNA makes proteins can be harnessed to carry out the tasks that underlie computing. Again, work is at an experimental level and the obstacles are enormous but bio-molecular computing demonstrates the way that nanotechnology challenges barriers between different scientific and technological disciplines.

DNA's negative electric charge means it can be exploited as a scaffold for creating nanoscale wires. Strands of DNA and conductive nanoparticles with a positive charge are incubated together. The attraction of negative to positive brings the two together to form wires, the length of which can be controlled by introducing enzymes that cut the DNA at determined points.

While quantum switch and bio-molecular computing are not likely to impinge on our lives for some years, if indeed they prove to have anything but niche applications, they do present potential paths not for bending Moore's laws but for entirely sidestepping them.

Nanotechnology goes to war

As with all scientific advances, the military has been quick to see the possibilities of nanotechnology. Indeed, there are few potential areas of application where the military is not implicated, be they transport, health care, communications or computing. Ostensibly civil applications are of interest to the military on three levels. First, and most mundanely, as a major employer of personnel and equipment the military forms communities within society that have logistical and personnel requirements similar to those of any large corporation, such as cheaper energy or more efficient transport and health care. Second, it can adapt technology developed in the laboratories of academia or corporations to its own purposes. Indeed, while the US Department of Defense is committed to maintaining a strong science programme of its own to ensure superiority over potential enemies, it is increasingly relying on the corporate and academic sectors to provide technological leadership and partnerships. Dual use may be as simple as adopting water-resistant clothing developed for use by campers or farmers, or more sophisticated, such as seeing the potential for improving the speed and manoeuvrability of armoured vehicles by reducing their weight while simultaneously strengthening the protection they provide to troops. Third, the military has its own special interests in nanotechnology, including the enhancement of existing weapons systems and the development of new armaments.

By 2004 the Pentagon was spending well over $300 million a year on nanotechnology research and expecting an increase in the budget. But the crossover between ostensibly civil and military research and development extends the reach of the military much further. The military works alongside and sponsors, or partners, other governmental, corporate and academic researchers, and ultimately provides a massive potential market for companies operating in the field. The US armed forces are some of the most aggressive seekers of patents for nanotechnology discoveries.

The National Aeronautics and Space Administration (Nasa), clearly part of the broad military–industrial complex, receives $34 million a year rising to $42 million a year under the 21st Century Nanotechnology Research and Development Act.[1] Under the Act the second biggest beneficiary, with appropriations ten times those of Nasa, is the US Department of Energy. The DoE has put nearly $3 million into work being done at West Michigan University to create an early-warning system for detecting chemical, biological and radiological weapons. The system is expected to be available by 2008–09.[2] Richard Smalley's Carbon Nanotechnologies took on a defence consultant back in 2002 specifically in order to help it market nanotubes to the US armed forces.[3] Along with Foster–Miller, it won a $3.96 million contract a couple of years later to produce a range of nanotube-based sealants for use on military aircraft.[4]

Under initiatives such as the Small Business Innovation Research programme and the Engineered Bio-molecular Nano-devices/ Systems programme, the Defense Sciences Office of the Defense Advanced Research Projects Agency (Darpa) offers funding for research into a variety of applications. In early 2005 Darpa contracted researchers at the University of Texas to develop nanotube muscles that would be chemically powered and much faster and stronger than their natural counterpart. These could lead to advanced artificial limbs for robots or amputees or feed into the project to build the super soldier of the near future.

Direct spending by the UK's Ministry of Defence has been trivial by comparison with the US, a mere £1.5 million a year.[5] The strategy is explicitly one of piggybacking on 'the international research community', sponsoring relatively inexpensive research in order to obtain key information 'both to determine [nanotechnology's] benefits for UK defence and to determine the threats that the technology might pose against the UK and its allies, recognising they may come in key areas more quickly than we think'. MOD-sponsored research is specifically geared towards collaboration with universities.

The military appreciation of the potential of nanotechnology began in the 1980s. By 2004 the Pentagon was spending $315 million a year on all nanotechnology-related research, according to Clifford Lau, senior science adviser at its office of basic research.[6] It was funding sixteen multimillion-dollar annual grants to university nanotechnology projects and another twenty-five under a multidisciplinary research programme. It was also spending $100 million on nanotechnology-related research in the field of information technology.

In 2001 a committee report written up for Nato,[7] the US-dominated military alliance, had concluded that new scientific advances, largely nanotechnology-based but including space weaponry and so-called nonlethal weapons, constituted a Revolution in Military Affairs (RMA), giving as a definition: 'a major change in the nature of warfare brought about by the innovative application of new technologies which, combined with dramatic changes in military doctrine and operational and organisational concepts, fundamentally alters the character and conduct of military operations.' To give a measure of the importance attached to the potential of the new advances, a list of previous RMAs is given: introduction of gunpowder and the development of the steam engine, the submarine, the internal combustion engine, the aeroplane and the atomic bomb.

'Nanotechnology is going to revolutionise everything we do', General Lester Lyles, commander of the US air force materiel command, told Congress in 2003.[8] In his 2001 Quadrennial Defense Review, US Secretary for Defence Donald Rumsfeld noted that, 'For the United States, the revolution in military affairs holds the potential to confer enormous advantages and to extend the current period of US military superiority.'

The doctrine of technical superiority is well established in US military thinking. Indeed it is well established in the modern iconography of Washington's military exploits of recent years. It is represented by the defunct Star Wars programme of the Reagan administration, resurrected by George W. Bush; the costly Stealth bombers of dubious efficiency; and the 'smart' bombs, possession of which did not prevent the hitting of a civilian air-raid shelter in Baghdad, the Chinese embassy in Belgrade, or the deaths of uncounted civilians during the invasion and occupation of Iraq.

And the determination to ensure US dominance through technology is echoed elsewhere. 'Unfortunately, while some progress has been made, the United States does not dominate nanotechnology', remarked Nick Smith, congressman for Michigan in 1999, as he opened a House of Representatives subcommittee session.[9]

There are three readily identifiable challenges to US military hegemony. The first is the type of peer competition that the Soviet Union posed. The prime candidate for such designation in the future is China, which is already engaged in competition with the

US for preferential access to the oil reserves of third parties. The second challenge comprises the so-called rogue states, a designation applied to all manner of developing-country states that present an obstacle to US dominance in their region but one which can, as Libya showed, rapidly be lifted to further US corporate and strategic interests. The third, of course, is the one that came to the fore with the 11 September 2001 attacks on New York and Washington, the non-state enemy.

The rethinking of US (and others') strategies in the wake of September 11 brought a new emphasis on the concept of 'homeland security'. The Office of Homeland Security was created. This soon permeated international trade and communications. With its Container Security Initiative, requiring extensive and early documentation of goods, on pain of delayed entry into the US, Washington pre-empted global maritime legislation and, in effect, exported its security frontline to the ports of trading partners on pain of damaging economic penalties. It also successfully insisted that foreign airlines hand over extensive details of passengers to the US authorities.

At the same time, scare stories about al-Qaeda sleeper cells proliferated. One recent book insisted:

> The sleeper agents, who are now among the American people, could be married to non-Muslims and living in spacious houses in the suburbs, or they could be single and living in inner-city apartment complexes. They could be attending Christian worship services on Sunday mornings and working as professionals in schools, hospitals, research facilities, chemical plants, nuclear energy facilities, and even government offices.[10]

While young Muslim suspects captured in Afghanistan were being incarcerated in Guantánamo Bay, Arab Americans were being interned inside the US. The fears – genuine or manfactured – of an enemy within and of the imminent possibility of modes of attack as unconventional as those launched against the Twin Towers – a 'dirty' bomb in a shipping container, widespread use of anthrax, sarin releases on public transport systems – opened up new opportunities for companies seeking to sell into the military establishment. As the security services opened a new front trawling for potential attackers and weapons inside North American and European cities, so the new emphasis on domestic security opened potential new markets for surveillance, monitoring and sensing equipment, among them nanotechnology providers. Indeed, a rather thoughtful book entitled *Nanotechnology and Homeland Security* by Daniel and Mark Ratner, two of the foremost commentators on nanoscience, provides numerous examples of ways in which nanotechnology could enhance security: 'In a world tainted by terrorism, the buildings likely to be targeted can and should participate in their own defense',[11] they say, going on to argue for more and better technology for the intelligence services, including the sort of decryption capability that nano-computing offers. 'What America and all the other nations of the free world need is an arsenal of "silver bullet" technologies'[12] to address the 'new' threats, they say.

The 2001 Quadrennial Defense Review explicitly picks out nanotechnology as one of the most promising paths for development, noting particularly that it 'may result in miniature, mobile, autonomous sensors that could penetrate the secure and remote facilities of an adversary'.

Sensor research has been well under way for some time. Under the rubric of Darpa, US corporation DynCorp had by 2000 completed preliminary testing of a 'gun-launched sensor carrier projectile for remote delivery and emplacement of MEMS (micro-electro-mechanical systems)-based sensors in a high-g environment'.[13]

The Moldice programme is particularly geared towards marrying up the sensing functions of biological systems with silicon circuitry to communicate information to the controller.

Notionally, the same qualities that allow nanoscale particles to identify viruses in the human body could enable them to alert a military command to the presence of enemy forces or particular weaponry. The battlefield of the future would be dusted with a coating of nanoscale sensors allowing precise identification of threats. (Of course, such intelligence only works if the enemy is not aware of it and capable of turning it against its user by feeding false data.) The US Congress was told in 2003 that:

> Already, DoD is developing 'smart dust', which are tiny robots the size of insects or even smaller. Although not quite nanotechnology, millions of these devices can be dropped into enemy territory to provide highly detailed surveillance. The potential application for even smaller, nanotechnology-based devices is even greater. Want to find Saddam Hussein or Osama bin Laden? Need to locate hidden weapons of mass destruction? Billions of essentially invisible spies could monitor every square inch of enemy territory, identify every person and every weapon, and even carry out missions to destroy enemy targets.[14]

The UK's Ministry of Defence says: 'Specially prepared clouds of nanotechnology particles could be used to disrupt electronic systems, affect the stealth characteristics of platforms flying through them and reduce the performance of communications and sensor systems.'[15]

While at the time of writing 'smart dust' was an aim not a reality, the smallest sensor devices in use being 'motes' the size of a bottletop, the threat-identification applications of nanoscience, first mentioned in this book in the context of medical diagnostics, are obvious. Companies such as Evident are developing 'a chip-based pathogen diagnosis system for clinical use that can be readily modified to detect trace amounts of anthrax, smallpox, plague and other possible biological weapons in the field or in the laboratory',[16] using semiconductor nanocrystals.

A key component of 'homeland security' is the protection not just of buildings but of a host of infrastructural facilities. There is little or no stretch from the current state of nanotechnology to one where all major installations are as standardly equipped with carpets or walls or windows that sense undesirable chemicals or bacteria as they are now with smoke alarms. One consultancy, which estimates the value of the major likely nanosensor markets in 2009 at almost $3 billion, estimates military and 'homeland' defence will account for over a third of the total.[17]

Technological superiority goes hand in hand with imperial conquest – the use of the Winchester carbine against Native Americans, the mowing down of Arab forces at Omdurman in 1898, the Kevlar-coated Israeli soldier backed by Apache gunships, the long-distance elimination of Iraqi army forces for minimal US and UK losses. The evolution of the US soldier continues into the realm of nanoscience, not least through the Institute for Soldier Technologies at Massachusetts Institute of Technology. The IST is funded by the US army and partnered by corporations such as Raytheon and DuPont. It has the mission to:

> use nanotechnology to dramatically improve the survival of soldiers. The ultimate goal is to create a 21st century battlesuit that combines high-tech capabilities with light weight and comfort. Imagine a bullet-proof jumpsuit, no thicker than ordinary spandex, that monitors health, eases injuries, communicates automatically, and maybe even lends superhuman abilities.[18]

This is part of the wider Future Force Warrior programme:

> to create a lightweight, overwhelmingly lethal, fully integrated individual combat system, including weapon, head-to-toe individual protection, netted communications, soldier worn power sources, and enhanced human performance. The program is aimed

at providing unsurpassed individual & squad lethality, survivability, communications, and responsiveness – a formidable warrior in an invincible team.[19]

Specific areas that the institute is working on include miniaturisation of communications equipment, lightweight clothing that adapts to weather conditions, ultra-lightweight body armour, clothing that adapts into casts for broken bones or acts as a tourniquet or delivers first aid, clothing that contains nanoscale sensors, even clothing that acts as an external muscle to increase a soldier's strength.

Information processing and communications are another major area of military interest in nanotechnology. Reference has already been made to the potential suitability of quantum and bio-molecular computing to encryption and decryption, which is clearly of importance not only to the military but to intelligence agencies, whether externally or domestically focused.

Darpa is pushing ahead with research into bio-molecular computing with a programme that aims to develop molecular devices that will chemically self-assemble into the required architecture. These nanoscale computers, small enough to sit en masse on the end of human hair, will yield massive gains in memory capacity, will clearly be deployable anywhere, will be cheap and, in part at least, self-assembling. They may well also offer the benefit of not being as vulnerable to electronic or radiation pulses as are traditional electronically based computers, a useful battlefield quality.

The military is also looking at the area of optical computing where data is transformed from electrical impulses into light. This is another area where nanotechnology will have much to offer in the medium to long term.

Concerns have been raised whether the revolution in military affairs that nanotechnology promotes will reach beyond battlefield capability and into the realms of military strategy. The debate is at the level of theory because it hypothesises developments that still look to be some way off, assuming they are ever realised.

The US government's National Defense University's house journal opined:

> In unconventional terms, bionanobots might be designed that, when ingested from the air by humans, would assay DNA codes and self destruct in an appropriate place (probably the brain) in those persons whose codes had been programmed. Nanobots could attack certain kinds of metals, lubricants, or rubber, destroying conventional weaponry by literally consuming it.[20]

The successful development by any military power of such weapons would constitute a breakthrough of enormous geopolitical significance because, like the atomic bomb, it would trump all pre-existing arms with the devastation that could be wrought on armed forces and civilians. Unlike conventional nuclear weapons (more precise, low-yield bombs are being worked on in the US), though, nanoweapons could be tailored to circumstances and so would be employable in small-scale wars or, indeed, in the control of an unruly populace.

So great a military advantage would potentially make or break global military dominance. In the hands of the US it would achieve the aim of maintaining superiority and undercutting any potential peer competitor. On the other hand, with research into nanotechnology being widely spread throughout the world, a breakthrough elsewhere could produce a new military superpower or give a client state like Israel unprecedented and dangerous bargaining power.

Mark Avrum Gubrud is one of only a handful of commentators to have taken an extended look at the wider implications of nanotechnology and military strategy.[21] He is sceptical about the development of the programmable genocidal bio-nanobot, pointing out that such a weapon would be dangerous to its creators, probably easy to defend against and of little use on an automated battlefield. But nanotechnology offers plenty of other 'colourful possibilities for creative mass murder', he says.

3

Timescales: from just around the corner to over the rainbow

Having surveyed some of the likely or potential applications of nanotechnology, it is worth spending a little time looking at the time frames involved. One of the fascinations of the new-wave technologies of which nanotechnology is part is that forecasts for applications can rapidly spin into the realms of science fiction as the theoretically possible gets muddled up with the imminently commercial. Having said that, there are many who argue that paradigm-shifting scientific advances are being made at a faster and faster rate, suggesting that our willingness to suspend disbelief – when reading about projects to build an elevator into space, or control our individual health through billions of nanobots in our bloodstream, or even replace manufacturing industry as we know it with nanofactories – should be recalibrated.

Of course, the advances made – 'accidental' penicillin-like discoveries apart – are not only a function of the state of scientific knowledge and equipment but also of the investment that goes into different branches of research and who controls that investment and to what end. Research and development only takes place to the extent that it empowers or enriches those who sponsor it. In much of the world, independent academic research is a thing of the past, with the university laboratory now a sponsored, branded profit centre dependent on industry or government agencies. That is not to say that guided research cannot bring results the consequences of which were never foreseen. The relationship between the political economy and technology is dialectical but not easily predictable.

At a more pedestrian level, the speed and direction of investment in nanotechnology are dictated by the appetite of investors, and that changes. In April 2004, one analyst specialising in the field wrote that the nascent industry was in a bind. It had promised the moon yet delivered to market only relatively unexciting incremental advances.[1] It needs to demonstrate its potential with a 'product shock', something that will make an impact in the imagination of the public and the investor community. Yet this requires taking risks at a time of investment risk aversity.

The rapidity and regularity with which advances are made in manipulating materials at the nanoscale and the number of laboratories engaged in research mean that obstacles to the deployment of nanotechnology in medicine or electronics or manufacturing are tumbling by the week. That means that even forecasts made as this book was being written might need revision by the time it is published. Nonetheless, the evaluations provide two things: first, a reality check on what is deemed likely in the short term, and second, some ideas of the possible economic value of nanotechnology in the next few years. This provides a basis for looking at the social implications of nanotechnology.

Applications on the cusp of commercialisation, by around 2010, are treated here as short term. Medium term is defined loosely as within ten to fifteen years and anything beyond that as long term. Looking across a range of sources there is broad agreement on the areas where nanotechnology is likely to impact first. This said, it must be borne in mind that a lot of the reports on nanotechnology are derivative, frequently citing the same relatively small pool of research. So, UK government documents cite US government figures and show little sign of independent investigation. Throughout the literature, a figure thrown out by the US National Nanotechnology Initiative that the nanotechnology market will be worth $1 trillion by 2015 is cited, probably more for its impact than its reliability. This highlights the broader definitional problems with nanotechnology discussed elsewhere.

On the cusp of commercialisation

The lab on a chip, enabling rapid diagnosis of illnesses, presence of bacteria in food processing, and environmental monitoring, is already available. In mid-2003 a chip cost £1,250 but the price was expected to tumble, making the tools much more widely available.[2] The market for the lab on a chip was forecast at a modest $60 million for 2005.[3] Looking at the broader market for medical devices and biotechnology products, the UK's Department of Trade and Industry quoted US government researchers who estimated that in 2002 nanotechnology's share was 1 per cent, $500 million in a $50 billion-a-year global market, but that it would double by 2005.[4] Its share of the 2003 $380-billion-a-year pharmaceutical products and delivery market was similar.

Development of improved photovoltaic cells through the use of nanotechnology has moved rapidly and looks certain to come to market in the short term. At the same time, the efficiency of fuel cells is improving both in terms of catalysis and storage of energy. The wider social and environmental potentials of these advances may be longer term but it is certain that the consumer electronics manufacturers will leap on them in the race for competitive advantage in products such as mobile phones. In the electronics industry the commercial impact of nanotechnology has been incremental rather than disruptive so far and that is likely to remain the case in the short term. CD players already utilise quantum well lasers but these have yet to hit the fibre optics communications market. The commercial introduction of carbon nanotube flat screens is imminent, as may be nanotube-based random access memory (RAM) in computing.[5] By 2004–05, the value of nanotechnology products in the electronics market was forecast to be £10–20 billion.[6] In late 2004, the German technology company Carl Zeiss began customer presentations of nanoscale lithography at a purpose-built laboratory, demonstrating the speed at which industry is getting to grips with the challenges of low-cost, systematic and reliable engineering of computer components at the nanoscale.

Sophisticated paints and coatings that exploit the properties of materials at the nanoscale to control heat loss or prevent fouling and rusting will see increasingly widespread development and use in the short term. This could have major implications for transports costs and energy saving by reducing the weight and the wear and tear on cars, planes and ships.

The Royal Society report, somewhat controversially given that it acknowledges serious concerns over the deployment of nano-particles into the environment, cites environmental remediation as a short-term area of application.[7] The ETC Group reports that agrochemical companies are in the process of patenting and even marketing pesticides employing emulsions with nanoscale droplets dispersed in a carrier liquid, the rationale being that they are better absorbed into the plants and less likely to clog equipment.[8]

Take-off time 2010

It looks as if the take-off point for nanotechnology will come towards 2010. It will be around that time that early applications come into general use and shares in respective markets become significant. That will encourage further uptake and standardisation, reducing costs and increasing financial incentives. At the same time, new applications, in the medical sector for example, will emerge from the trial phase and become commercially available, while advances at the research level will give further pointers to yet more applications.

A study of the car industry in 2004 pointed out a string of benefits nanomaterials offer to manufacturers. Reduction of the use of rare metals in catalytic converters could bring savings of $1 billion a year. More accurate engineering could reduce rejection of parts, saving $2.5 billion a year. Weight savings of up to 25 per cent, with consequent fuel efficiency benefits, would produce major advantages. Yet in 2004, penetration of nanotechnology into the automotive industry was valued at a paltry $1.1 billion due to paucity of commercial products, high prices because of lack of economies of scale, and low end-user awareness. However, this was set to change, the study argued. Nanotechnology would be used in 70 per cent of automotive applications by 2015 with revenues rising to $6.46 billion. By 2008, vehicle electronics would be employing nanotechnology, following on from paints and functional surfaces and lightweight structures such as those already being deployed by General Motors.[9]

The use of sensors exploiting nanoscale science, for everything from military and security purposes to transport ergonomics and early detection of cancers, is projected to be worth $2.7 billion by 2008 but gaining momentum enough to reach over $17 billion four years later, with tenfold increases in the automotive and aviation industries according to one industry report.[10]

The ETC report referred to above cites a US company that expects to be building sensors the size of an aspirin or a grain of rice within a few years, with a price tag of just a few dollars each. The company's current 'motes' are the size of a bottletop and have been used to monitor the performance of oil tankers, wildlife habitats, stress on bridges, and grocery stores, and are to be tested for use in port security. ETC envisages their deployment by agro-industry to monitor crop growth.

The RAND evaluation of new technologies for the US National Intelligence Council talks of

> A world with pervasive, networked sensors and actuators (e.g. on and part of walls, clothing, appliances, vehicles, and the environment) [that] promises to improve, optimise, and customise the capability of systems and devices through availability of information and more direct actuation.[11]

Indeed, this generally sober document envisages by 2015 clothes that respond to weather, interface with information systems and protect wounds – all clearly tied into the sort of military research discussed earlier. 'Low profile' biometric sensor use by the police and military is also seen as likely by this point. This is in addition to applications such as buildings and infrastructure that can sense and respond to changes in the weather or to damage, and a plethora of consumer applications.

By 2015–20, the electronics industry and the medical sector will well and truly have entered the nano-age. After 2010, the speculative values put on the market for nanotechnology-enabled information technology and electronics begin to look enormous – £70 billion a year with impressive annual growth rates, according to a forecast cited by the British government. The growth rate for micro- and nanotechnology in telecommunications is 70 per cent.[12] Assuming nanotechnology is harnessed successfully by the semiconductor industry through processes such as step and flash imprint lithography and making use of new nanoscale polymers, annual production from nanotechnology in that industry could reach $300 billion a year well before 2020,[13] although this might be ambitious given that some industry analysts do not envisage nanoscale commercial semiconductors becoming significant before 2012.[14] Additionally, some commentators have estimated it would take a decade for the industry to retool.

This shift to dependence on nanoscale technology in the electronics industry will nonetheless be within the parameters of pre-nanotechnology computing paradigms. Around 2015 is the timescale by which molecular computing might begin to come into its own, if aided by progress in reliable, consistent and cheap self-assembly processes. This is what the RAND report refers to as: 'the longer-term, traditionally elusive question in the period after 2015 … how long will traditional silicon computing last? And when, if ever, will a competing technology become available and attractive?'[15] The Royal Society sees quantum-switch cryptography replacing current methods before 2015, but this is a niche application. Hewlett-Packard, the US technology group, however, believes its nanoscale 'crossbar latches', which it believes could supersede the conventional transistor, could be commercially viable by 2012.

In the medical field, extensive clinical trials mean the introduction (or rejection) of new procedures and materials takes a long time. But by 2010–20 targeted drug delivery and better medical implants and artificially created organs are expected to have entered commercial use.[16] By 2015–20, the US National Science Foundation sees about half of the $180-billion-a-year pharmaceuticals production industry deriving from nanotechnology.[17] The Royal Society notes the potential for a range of medical applications including gene therapy, cancer treatment, nanoceramics and nanoelectronics in prosthetics but, as noted elsewhere, is less bullish than some, seeing these applications as being long-term possibilities rather than medium-term certainties.[18]

In the energy sector, imminent developments in the fields of solar power and fuel cells are likely to become increasingly important. The far end of the medium-term time frame is where the car industry sees the hydrogen fuel cell replacing petrol. At the same time, light-emitting diodes will contribute significantly to energy saving.

A necessary driver to the widespread use of discoveries made in the laboratory is the development of techniques to manufacture products from nanoscale particles. It is of little practical use being able to create new forms of ceramic or nanotube composites or sensors or computer switching if it can only be done one atom at a time by highly trained technicians using highly expensive equipment such as scanning tunnelling microscopes. In the next five to fifteen years simple self-assembly and directed assembly of materials is widely forecast. This will require progress not only in the techniques of assembly but also in the tools needed to measure, model and quality-control materials. According to the Royal Society, the biotechnology and information technology industries are likely to be the early users of these first macroscale products created from self- or directed assembly of nanoscale materials. However, the initial cost of such materials is expected to be very high, perhaps $1 million a tonne with annual global production of no more than 10,000 tonnes at the very most. Indeed the Royal Society argues that prices could stay high because 'though the effect of the nanomaterial will be to add value to consumer products, it will only form a tiny fraction of the final product as sold.'[19]

Estimates of the overall market value of nanotechnology now and in the future depend, of course, both on the definition used for nanotechnology and on assumptions of the speed at which laboratory techniques can be commercialised, the latter depending not only on development of economies of scale but also on issues around patenting, industry regulation and public acceptance.

The nice round estimate of $1 trillion by 2015 used by various government agencies in the US and adopted by the NanoBusiness Alliance there has already been mentioned. Research by DG Bank is more cautious, assessing the value at €50 billion in 2002 with an annual growth rate of over 25 per cent. It extrapolates a 2010 value of €220 billion, with growth rates accelerated to 20–30 per cent a year.[20] The UK government cites a financial house's estimate of a 2005 value of £105 billion but then seems to fall back on US-generated figures of £500 billion by 2008, £700 billion by 2010 and then the omnipresent $1 trillion by 2015.[21]

Leaving aside the question of whether definitions of nanotechnology have been broadened and forecasts of value exaggerated by players interested in securing funding from investors and governments, the scale of the figures needs putting in some perspective. The turnover of the global semiconductor industry in 2004 was in excess of $200 billion.[22] That of the pharmaceuticals industry is of the same order. The automotive industry's turnover is nearer $1 trillion and it employs 8 million people, meaning that if it were a national economy it would be the sixth largest in the world.

Using the figures of €50 billion for 2002 and €200 billion by 2010, the value of nanotechnology equated to something like the 2002 gross domestic product of Bangladesh for the first date and that of Norway for the second. The $1 trillion projection equates to just less than the combined gross domestic product of all low-income countries in 2002, something over the GDP of central and eastern Europe and the Commonwealth of Independent States, and substantially more than the income of South Asia in 2002.[23]

Beyond the horizon

Going beyond a fifteen- or twenty-year timescale for technology is to go beyond the realm of forecasts and into the realm of visions.

Some of these are the dream and nightmare visions of the prophets of nanotechnology, some are much narrower conceptions of more specific objectives or products derived from current understanding of the properties of some materials at the nanoscale. Just a taste of these is given here.

One example of the latter is the elevator to the stars. The strength and light weight of carbon nanotubes has encouraged Nasa to plough $500,000 into initial research for the project, with another $2.5 billion earmarked. It envisages a hollow cable of nanotubes a metre wide with paper-thin walls and capable of supporting a weight of 13 tonnes. This would carry a payload more than 60,000 miles into space, enabling cheap space travel and deployment of materiel. The project's director believes he could have an early version in operation as early as 2020 at a cost of $10 billion – well below the finance committed to other space projects.[24]

For some, a developed interface between computing and biology using nanotechnology is the prospect of coming decades. Entrepreneur and inventor Ray Kurzweil argues that we are on an accelerating journey of technical advance. The overall rate of technical progress – the 'paradigm shift rate' – is doubling every decade, he says, so the twenty-first century will see massively more and massively faster change than did the twentieth, let alone the nineteenth. This being his viewpoint, Kurzweil believes a 'golden age of nanotechnology' is rather nearer than do others, and:

> This era will bring us the ability to essentially convert software i.e. information, directly into physical products.... Computers will have greater computational capacity than the human brain, and we will be completing the reverse engineering of the human brain to reveal the software design of human intelligence ... With the advent of nanotechnology, we will be able to keep our bodies and brains in a healthy, optimal state indefinitely.[25]

A conference organised by by the Foresight Institute ran the gamut of visions and fears of the not-so-distant future. One speaker, looking ahead no further than 2025, envisaged powerful, low-energy computers that would fit in the frame of a pair of spectacles; nanoclinics for those living some distance from hospitals, containing diagnostics, medicines and preventive treatments; and refineries capable of breaking down any unwanted items from sewage to household goods into component chemicals that could be reused by nanofactories.[26]

4

Investment:

owning the keys to the kingdom

Control of research, development and ownership of intellectual property rights for any new technology is key to profiting from its commercialisation and, indeed, to determining its application. At the strategic level that gives governments an interest in ensuring that institutions under their jurisdiction and companies subject to their influence are not left behind in the race to exploit technologies that offer military advantages or economic benefits.

At the commercial level it means companies need to evaluate the potential of new technologies for their industries and then decide the best strategy for exploiting that potential. That strategy will be based on choices of how to access research, options for securing – and, preferably, profiting from – patents, and decisions about the most profitable applications. To be more concrete, for a pharmaceuticals company it would entail deciding whether to do the research in-house or work with a specialist partner, commercial or academic. Then it would entail patenting discoveries and calculating whether it was most profitable to reap fees from letting others employ the discoveries or keep them for sole use for as long as possible. For the potential end user, the crucial decision would be which illnesses or conditions it was deemed most profitable to treat and at what price.

The battle to force drug companies to provide relatively affordable treatment to HIV/Aids sufferers in the developing world highlighted the pharmaceutical industry's determination to defend profit maximisation for as long as possible, with only the threat to market share posed by manufacturers of generic drugs forcing them into a partial climbdown. Miles White, chief executive of US pharmaceuticals group Abbott Laboratories, is open about why he supports so-called corporate citizenship initiatives to send HIV/Aids treatments to Africa while hiking prices in the US:

> Why spend money on corporate citizenship? Frankly because it's required. If I don't provide our products in Africa, governments will license our intellectual property to others who can. Governments will intervene. Make no mistake, they will do that … If Africa does it, why not China? Why not India? Why not Latin America?[1]

As if to underline the point, a few months later Brazil was on the verge of invoking special-exception trade regulations to break several patents on HIV/Aids drugs.

It is, of course, the rich countries of the world and the corporations domiciled there that dominate emerging technologies, and those technologies conspire to maintain the wealth and power of those nations and corporations. That said, research into nanotechnology is relatively widespread, with some of the major developing countries as well as Russia and countries of eastern Europe engaging in work. Because nanotechnology is a new tier of science, crossing the boundaries of traditional disciplines and having potential applications across every industrial and service sector, just as electronics does, the scope for research and development is vast. This, combined with ever-improving global communications and the education and training of the intellectual elites of developing countries in industrialised countries, means there are distinct possibilities that some developing countries will be able to establish themselves as niche players, establishing specialist clusters of technological expertise whether home-grown or simply outposts of foreign corporations.

There is an emerging geographic specialisation in nanotechnology already. In a survey, venture capital company 3i found the US coming out on top in nanotechnology work in every industry, but when the US was split into regions a more complex pattern emerged, with respondents considering Japan the leader in electronic applications, Germany in chemical applications, the US West Coast in medical, material and manufacturing. South Korea and Taiwan achieved rankings of four or five for electronics and manufacturing applications.[2]

Despite the international reach of so many corporations and their increasing ability to swap sourcing of materials, labour and services from country to country, some other national characteristics remain evident. In the US, the UK and Germany, venture capital has dominated non-governmental investment in nanotechnology start-up companies, whereas in Japan almost all nanotechnology venture investments have been established by industrial groups setting up their own captive companies.[3] In the US and Japan the proportion of investment in nanotechnology accounted for by business rather than government is higher than in Europe.[4]

Governmental spending spree

The US provoked a flurry of national campaigns to boost nanotechnology research after Washington hiked its spend from $245 million in 2000 to $465 million in 2001 and unveiled the multidisciplinary National Nanotechnology Initiative. For 2005, a figure of $886 million was projected, excluding direct military funding, which adds another third, and state-level funding. The latter can be substantial, as in New York's $75 million contribution towards a $400 million centre-of-excellence project with IBM and chip maker ASML. Washington's investment in nanotechnology is set to exceed massively its funding for the Human Genome Project.[5] In the US budget for 2006, overall funding for nanotechnology was slightly reduced but was held by industry to have fared well compared to other discretionary areas of spending that were not purely military. That said, to keep the investment in context, nano-technology represents only some 3 per cent of US government R&D spending.[6]

Between 1997 and 2000 research and development spend reported by government agencies worldwide doubled to $925 million, but between 2000 and 2003 it more than trebled to over $3 billion.[7] From 2001 most industrialised countries had set up coordinated national strategies on one model or another, often determined by the customary interrelationship between govern-ment, academia and industry. Most of the funding made available by governments is to support R&D in a fast-moving area that is seen as being on the verge of larger scale commercialisation. Taiwan is something of an exception in that the bulk of its government spend is on industrialization of nanotechnology.

Indeed, the enthusiasm in Washington, which was, of course, underlined by the increased funding in the 2003 Act, seems to have prompted concerns in some countries that they and 'their' companies were losing out to foreign competition. By 2004, a committee of the UK parliament was excoriating in its criticism of government, saying it was 'culpable of failing to build on an early successful nanotechnology programme in the 1980s' and that 'the levels of investment planned are insufficient to match those

of other major international competitors',[8] and this despite the
warnings given in an earlier report published in 2001.

At the European Union level, the same worries are apparent.
A communiqué of 2004 stated:

> Over the last decade the European Union has established a strong
> knowledge base in nanosciences. Our ability to maintain this posi-
> tion is in doubt since the EU is investing proportionately less than
> its main competitors and lacks world-class infrastructure ('poles of
> excellence') that muster the necessary critical mass. This is despite
> the fact that investment in national EU programmes is growing in
> a rapid but independent way.[9]

The same document compared per capita spend on nanotechnology
in the US, Japan and the EU (including the ten new member states),
finding it to be €3.7, €6.2 and €2.4, respectively, in 2004.[10]

Concern about losing competitive advantage to the US was also
evident in Japan, which had led R&D in the early 1990s, where:

> Typically, there are also fears that in nanotechnology, Japan is being
> left behind. Equally typically, these fears relate exclusively to the
> US – the launch of the National Technology Initiative by the
> Clinton administration with an initial funding of $270 million ...
> has exacerbated these fears.[11]

At least thirty countries had started up national nanotechnology
initiatives by 2003. Government agency spends in that year in
Western Europe were estimated at $650 million, in the US $774
million, in Japan $800 million (so much for falling behind the
US), and elsewhere in the world another $800 million.[12]

Within the EU, Germany planned to spend £201 million in
2005, maintaining its place as biggest government investor in nanotechnology research in the grouping, with France committing well
over £100 million a year for four years. UK central government
spend would be only £45 million a year.

The established big players of the industrialised world also look with concern towards potential competitors elsewhere, particularly in developing Asia. China, viewed as the major potential economic and strategic threat of the future, is catching up with the US and the EU in terms of the scientific literature it produces around nanotechnology – publication trends are considered a good measure of R&D effort. One estimate is that Chinese government support for nanotechnology is around £100 million a year with non-government investment for the last ten years amounting to almost £2.2 billion.[13] Others have estimated China's investment rate as much higher than this and have pointed out that such levels of expenditure in a developing country buy a lot more than they would in an OECD country.

Taiwan's government has a declared target of becoming a regional centre of nanotechnology production within a decade. Some $700 million of government funding has been pledged over five years, with over half committed to industrialisation rather than R&D. The national Nanotechnology Research Centre forecasts Taiwan's output to be worth $29 billion by 2010, representing 3 per cent of global production. Materials and chemicals are expected to account for over 40 per cent of the country's nanotechnology-related production in 2008, with electronics reaching 35 per cent and metals and machinery the balance. Some sixty companies have committed over $5.5 billion towards manufacturing operations at Taichung Science Park, dubbed Nano City.[14]

South Korea has begun a $2 billion publicly funded programme[15] and Singapore has identified nanotechnology as an important future area of growth. India has a number of institutes actively engaged in research and is likely to follow up its success in developing computer software clusters with nanoscience clusters. It has signed a cooperation agreement with Israel.

Shimon Peres, former Israeli prime minister, has identified new technology as an area of great economic importance to the Israeli state, saying it promises bigger returns than agriculture and industry combined. But he also ties it explicitly to strategic concerns, writing:

> Forty-five years ago … I had the opportunity to develop a nuclear option for the State of Israel. At the time, many looked upon this initiative with skepticism. Today, we know its importance.
>   The pursuit of nanotechnology is an extension of the nuclear policy in a constructive form. Israel needs to make a superhuman effort once again and join this new global trend, so as to secure itself a seat in the first row of participants.[16]

The Israeli government had already invested some $150 million in nanotechnology by the end of 2003, but the plan hatched by Peres and his venture capitalist son was to seek twice this amount from US donors, thus accessing free capital and forging further technological links between Israel and its superpower sponsor.[17]

Corporate strategies

For an established manufacturer a number of factors are likely to be considered when deciding whether or how to approach investment in nanotechnology. There will be an evaluation of the extent to which the processes employed by the company and the markets it sells into will be affected. Does nanotechnology offer only incremental benefits in terms of efficiency of production or will it revolutionise the process, replacing costly workers and equipment with guided self-assembly? Does it hold out a realistic prospect of rendering current products redundant or simply opening up new niche markets that the company may decide to forgo? The electronics industry faces this question as it addresses whether nanotechnology will provide a lifeline for silicon-based computing by facilitating more and more accurate lithography, or a wholly new industry paradigm with entirely new computing architecture. If the latter, at what point is it no longer worthwhile spending billions of dollars building new silicon-based semiconductor plants?

To make a hard and fast decision on these issues would be dangerous given the speed of development of nanotechnology, on the one hand, and the enormous remaining challenges, on the other. So, for many larger companies an obvious strategy is to maintain a relatively cheap watching brief, committing just enough resources to ensure that existing market share is not going to be eclipsed overnight. A chemicals industry publication put it this way as late as September 2003:

> Major chemical firms are very much aware of what is happening in the nanotech field, but most say they are still trying to figure out where nanotechnology and nanomaterials fit into their products and existing businesses. While trying to decide their strategy, companies are beginning to develop their own technical expertise or to tap into it externally.[18]

Monitoring and participating in 'disruptive technologies' that threaten or promise to transform corporations' existing markets is, of course, normal business practice. The oil and car-making industries have strategies for dealing with the replacement of petrol-fuelled vehicles, something seen as occurring on a significant scale in the next fifteen years or so. Royal Dutch/Shell works with General Motors to demonstrate the viability of hydrogen cars and refuelling infrastructure. It also has a range of partner-ships for the development of fuel cell technology and hydrogen purification and storage. Through Chrysalix Energy in Canada it has a venture capital arm to invest in promising fuel cell start-up companies. Another partner in Chrysalix is Ballard Power Systems, perhaps the best-known fuel cell developer. Ballard's development as a (small) company has been driven by its 'alliance' with car giants Daimler-Chrysler and Ford. The car makers invested in Ballard to access its research and development and in late 2004 bought out its vehicle fuel cell systems business and further tied the company to themselves.

Shell and its rival BP are also major players in the development of solar technology, just as in the past oil companies hedged their bets with sizeable investments in coal mining. Both fuel cell and solar energy, of course, are important areas of interest for nano-technology researchers.

There are times when governments have become concerned that 'their' industrial companies are lagging behind those based in other countries, thus endangering national economic (and strategic) ambitions. In the US, Japan and Germany corporate investment began to ramp up some time after 1998, probably triggered by US government interest and funding. Others were slow to keep up. The parliamentary committee advising the UK government was concerned as recently as early 2003 that:

> few large UK companies were using, or had any real strategy for adopting nanotechnology. In the main, large companies regarded nanotechnology as somewhat peripheral to their core business, but expressed an increasing anxiety about their lack of information on its potential for product improvement or development. UK companies were found to be slow to identify or adopt 'disruptive technologies' which require moving away from traditional approaches.[19]

Anglo-Dutch food giant Unilever showed an early interest but even there the company had only invested some £5 million in nanotechnology of a total R&D spend of many hundreds of millions at that point.[20] Pharmaceuticals company GlaxoSmithKline and armaments company Qinetiq were other early movers.

While biotechnology's implications are enormous, its spread is over a relatively discrete group of industries, primarily agriculture, food processing and pharmaceuticals. But nanotechnology is a mode of operating, a new level of processing and producing that potentially reaches across every sector. To that extent it is more like the introduction of computing, which reaches into design, manufacture, administration, finance, sales and servicing.

So, a manufacturer needs also to assess the range of applications nanotechnology may have for the industry. For example, for a car maker nanotechnology offers new materials for body panels, new forms of lubrication based on nanoscale bearings, additives to existing fuels, advances in alternative fuel technology, and new displays – just to mention a few actual or likely developments. The costs of research and development (which might fail) and then commercialisation and likely payback time must be evaluated.

The second half of the 1990s saw the inflation of the dotcom bubble, which was to burst dramatically in 2000. In retrospect (and at the time, for some observers) the tendentiousness of the dotcom proposition was obvious. A number of companies floated on stock exchanges, raising large amounts of capital and trading at inflated prices having never turned a profit. The barrier to entry into the market was low, with little investment required to set up a company that often produced nothing but was simply an alternative medium for marketing and selling. Losses were accepted as the price for winning market share when the existence of a viable market was often unproven.

When the collapse came it rebounded across the technology sector, hitting telecoms and computing as well as the dotcoms. The technology-weighted index of the Nasdaq exchange in the US, which soared from 1,000 to 5,000 points between 1996 and 2000, collapsed to around 2,500 in 2000 and kept on falling (aided no doubt by the effects of the September 11-induced downturn) to under 1,500 for part of 2002 before recovering somewhat to around 2,000 in 2004.

This experience has left a legacy fear of 'hype', the inflation of commercial potential in order to secure finance. Indeed, it has been suggested that some companies involved in the practical application of nanotechnology have been keen to downplay its potential in order to exclude any possible charge of hyping, which might provoke a flight of capital before the industry has even taken off. Nanotechnology proponents argue that the emerging nanotechnology sector is not similar to the dotcom sector of the 1990s. In the first place, there is a real, physical product, not a service of unproven interest. Then, where the threshold to entry to the dotcom world was low, for nanotechnology the individuality of a product is identifiable and can be patented, development periods are relatively long, there is a finite product on offer, and the cost of R&D limits entry. Also, the threshold of consumer acceptance of a dotcom product was arguably high – why use this website rather than that one and, indeed, why order by computer rather than telephone? Unless public concerns over nanotechnology balloon, there is unlikely to be resistance (assuming prices to be comparable) to a new tool for identifying a disease or an energy-saving windowpane, a super-efficient water filter or lighter and stronger vehicle part. (Environmental 'remediation' techniques or food labelling might excite more immediate concerns.) That said, it should be remembered that one of the major inhibitors to headlong investment by companies has been lack of clarity over likely applications and uncertainty about whether nanotechnology offers something qualitatively better at a justifiable cost.

Looking at a sample of multinational companies, the range and mix of tactics for ensuring access to progress in nanotechnology is evident. Employment of in-house and outsourced R&D ensures that the corporations that dominate pharmaceuticals, car making, armaments, chemicals and energy, and information technology will maintain their grip as new technologies emerge. Some major new players may emerge in the way that Microsoft ballooned in the software business, but the overwhelming majority of specialist start-up companies will be subsumed, unable to compete or swallowed up by established corporations. That is not to say that nanotechnology may not force major restructuring on some of the giant companies – just as the eruption of biotechnology forced a series of takeovers, mergers, demergers and spin-offs in the chemical and pharmaceuticals industries as they accommodated and exploited the emergent 'life science' business. Indeed, there are already small examples of the nanotechnology interests of a company being hived off into a subsidiary: Nanocor, which specialises in the dispersal of nanoparticles of specialist clay to change the properties of other materials, was created out of the nanotechnology interests of speciality mineral producer Amcol in the US.

The German chemical group BASF provides an example of corporate strategy towards nanotechnology. In-house, BASF has developed hyperbranched polymers with a wide variety of applications, including particularly adhesive printing inks and tougher and more flexible automotive coatings. It is also working on cube-shaped nanostructures for storing hydrogen. These could be used with fuel cells to replace conventional batteries in micro-electronic equipment. Surface coatings based on the nanoscale properties of the lotus leaf were ready for marketing in 2004. Alongside this in-house work, BASF has a venture capital subsidiary that gives it a window onto the work of niche and start-up companies. This led it to invest in Oxonica, a spin-off company of Oxford University. That led to a BASF partnership with Cerulean, a subsidiary of Oxonica, to develop and market a motor fuel additive.

Air Products, the large US-based specialist gas and chemical producer, provides another example of a major company using partnerships and investments to exploit new technologies. It established a joint venture with chemicals corporation Dupont in 2001 to sell nanoscale materials to semiconductor manufacturers. It has invested in a niche company with a proprietary metal and metal oxide nanoparticle production technology. In 2004 it began a joint venture with Nanogate Technologies of Germany, which specialises in creating stable dispersions of inorganic nanoparticles to provide customised properties such as transparency or water resistance. Air Products also partners venture capital funds to tap into developments in nanotechnology, having relationships with specialist funds Inverness Capital and NGEN.[21]

Oil company Conoco Phillips has a joint venture with Oklahoma University to manufacture nanotubes, which it sees having applications in designing materials for the construction of lighter and stronger offshore drilling equipment. Chevron Texaco's subsidiary Molecular Diamond Technologies came out of the accidental discovery of a particular form of diamondoid that could have applications in a range of fields from motor oil to microprocessing. Apache, an expanding US independent oil company, has an agreement with a company developing sensor technology for oil field exploration.[22]

A more direct approach into the heart of nanomaterial manufacturing was evident in the establishment of Frontier Carbon by Mitsubishi Chemical and Nanotech Partners, a venture fund set up by Mitsubishi Corporation. Frontier Carbon was established in 2001 with the aim of becoming the first mass producer of fullerenes or 'buckyballs'. Its output, according to the Nanotech Partners website in late 2004, was 40 tonnes a year, well short of the 1,500 tonnes foreseen when it was set up (a target put back to 2007), but nonetheless dwarfing the output of other producers. Its economies of scale meant it could aggressively cut prices to $5 per gram for mixed fullerenes.

Start-up companies and venture capital

Particularly in the US but elsewhere as well start-up nanotechnology companies have frequently emerged from the research done in academic institutions. The scientific expertise of the founders may be invaluable but few start-ups are likely to grow into large-scale companies because anything commercially viable they have to offer will be gobbled up by bigger players through partnerships, investment, straight buy-outs, or the licensing of technology.

Establishing with any accuracy just how many nanotechnology start-up companies there are at any given time is as slippery a task as defining nanotechnology. Nonetheless, finance house JP Morgan put the number in existence or in incubation in the US in 2003 at around 1,000 (a tenfold increase on three years before), and estimated this to be about a half of the global total.[23] The directory of the US Nanobusiness Alliance has some 700 entries, while NanoInvestor News was tracking some 960 companies at the beginning of 2005.

A major challenge for start-up companies is funding, both seed capital and then cash to see the company through to commercialisation of its products. In applications where adoption is likely to be quick (often because the product enhances an existing line in the way dirt resistance enhances existing paints or textiles) the funding stream is obviously shorter, but the likelihood of being taken over by a bigger company is greater. But, as the 3i report pointed out, in the extreme example of a drug, where regulation is particularly tight, it can take sixteen years from discovery to market delivery. The chances of a small company holding out that long are infinitesimal.

Because few nanotechnology companies are stock-market listed it is not easy to gauge the finances of even the better-known niche players but few, even of the respected companies, are yet making money. Listed on the Nasdaq exchange in New York, Nanophase Technologies made a loss of $1.7 million in the third quarter of 2004; Kopin made a loss of $1.1 million in the same period. Altair Nanotech made a nine-month loss of $5.3 million to the end of the third quarter of 2004. By contrast, NVE, which is developing flash memory chips using nanotechnology, turned a profit of $400,000 in its second quarter of its fiscal 2005 year. These sums are pitifully small when contrasted with the $100 million that IBM alone has committed to research on nanoelectronics.

The model that nanotechnology start-ups follow is likely to be that of the biotechnology industry, where of hundreds that were established only seventeen reached sustainable profitability between 1986 and 1999.[24] The start-ups provided innovation but their survival quickly came to depend on contracts, joint ventures, investment deals, licensing and marketing agreements with big pharmaceuticals, food and chemical corporations.[25]

Venture capital is the obvious path for finding funds in the absence of government grants. JP Morgan reckoned that more than sixty venture capital firms in the US, aside from the venture capital funds established by corporations, had invested in nanotechnology projects by 2003.[26] These ranged from the likes of JP Morgan itself and 3i, with a widespread portfolio of interests, through to new technology specialists such as NGEN which is backed by a range of multinationals that can use their financial input either as a straight investment or as a means to scout for partners or takeover targets. Venture capital investment in nanotechnology was some $250–300 million in 2002, according to one estimate,[27] and $500 million according to another.[28] The figure for 2003 was put at $301 million, according to newsletter *Small Times*, falling significantly to under $200 million in 2004. However, the fourth quarter of the year showed a marked recovery and the number of companies funded rose markedly over previous years.[29]

Becoming a publicly traded company by floating shares on a stock market is another route to financing. However, this is open to few start-up companies without an established commercial record, particularly after the disastrous flotations of the dotcom boom and bust and then the global equity market collapse that followed the September 11 attacks on the US. The flotation route is a tricky one requiring the right company, pitched in the right way at just the right time. Indeed, the decision of industry darling Nanosystems in 2004 to withdraw its proposed flotation prompted a debate on whether this was a signal of lack of investor confidence in the company or in nanotechnology start-ups as a class or just a reflection of a less than bullish equity market. The Nanobusiness Alliance was even moved to issue a statement noting the general market conditions, the lack of market familiarity with companies like Nanosystems, and counterproductive media use of the company as a bell-wether for the nascent sector. Nanosystems' semiconductor nanocrystal technology was closer to commercial breakthrough than many established biotech companies, the statement argued.

The *NanoInvestor News* website lists some 160 companies as publicly traded nanotechnology companies, but a high proportion were broader, household-name multinationals with an interest in nanotechnology, ranging from Swiss engineer ABB to Xerox. Merrill Lynch has started an index to track the performance of the nanotechnology industry, using only companies that have a significant percentage of future profits tied to nanotechnology. The handpicked list comprises twenty-five companies.

Another route to financing is the patenting and then licensing of company discoveries and inventions. In this way, even small companies may control and profit from fragments of knowledge perhaps gleaned incidentally from work in a university laboratory. In isolation the fragments may be worthless but for another company they may be a vital piece of a jigsaw that makes up a product or a process. That gives them a market value that can be traded in for licence fees or partnerships with other companies. The number of patents won is regarded as a measure of success by companies large and small. Lauding a young researcher, General Motors noted, 'Since joining General Motors in 1994, he has six patents under his belt.'[30] One of the measures of the promise of Nanosystems (mentioned above) was that it had some 250 patents approved and applied for.

For those companies not in a position to exploit their own research findings, earnings from licensing out patented knowledge offer a finance stream that may support other activity. However, the licensees are likely to be bigger, stronger, richer players, and the experience of the biotechnology industry may once again provide the model for nanotechnology. There, as more and more patents were controlled by big companies, the industry became more and more characterised by cross-licensing and inter-company agreements, networks, alliances and joint ventures.

> Arrangements between companies work by a process of give and take and smaller companies may not have enough to bring to the negotiating table. Some commentators even suspect that larger companies may be seeking increased regulation of genetically engineered plants in order to create competitive disadvantages for smaller more innovative firms.[31]

In 1990, some 50 per cent of plant patent applications in the EU were from just eight companies.[32]

5

The threat

A similar problem could arise from the threat of nanotechnology to natural resources, on a scale comparable only to that of nuclear accidents. If set free uncontrolled, nano robots could, with the necessary constant power supply, transform organic substances in the environment into new materials or penetrate into the soil, causing permanent damage to crop cells or even destroying them. These would be totally new loss scenarios, likely to go far beyond anything experienced up to now in today's hi-tech world.[1]

As technology brings benefits and prosperity to its users, it may leave others behind and create new class disparities. Although technology will help alleviate some severe hardships (e.g. food shortages and nutritional problems in the developing world), it will create real economic disparities both between and within the developed and developing worlds.[2]

The two statements above are drawn not from environmental campaigning groups or the labour movement but from one of the world's leading insurance companies and from a paper prepared for the US National Intelligence Council. They lead us into an examination of some of the concerns that nanotechnology raises for the environment, society and the individual. There are a small number of non-governmental organisations devoting all or much of their time to stimulating debate about nanotechnology. These are not Luddite groups. Indeed a founder of the Foresight Institute was none other than Eric Drexler, apostle of Feynman and molecular manufacturing visionary. The foreword of a paper commissioned by Greenpeace noted that:

> New technologies feature prominently in our ongoing campaigns against genetic modified crops and nuclear power; however, they are also an integral part of our solutions to environmental problems, including renewable energy technologies, such as solar, wind and wave power, and waste treatment technologies, such as mechanical–biological treatement.[3]

Some, like the ETC Group, are highly critical of the path along which nanotechnology is being allowed to develop. But generally they concur that the most pressing need is for much wider knowledge and discussion about nanotechnology. The foreword to the Greenpeace study also noted the problem in locating speakers who could talk with authority on new technologies or their political and economic impact. Indeed, the debate, the research and the literature around nanotechnology are strikingly limited. The same names of the same cliques of exponents crop up again and again – Drexler, Roco, Merkle, Smalley. Government, corporate and institutional reports fall back on the same old estimates of future market size and development – that $1 trillion figure.

Unexcited by the day-to-day laboratory advances and their development into goods on shelves, media reports either focus on the science-fiction threats and spectacular promises – the 'grey goo' menace adopted to great media excitement by Britain's Prince Charles or the cancer cure round the corner.

Without doubt there is a place for consideration of the more distant or far-fetched issues around nanotechnology, but what is needed now is, first, an awareness in civil society across the globe of the creep of nanotechnology into the lives of workers and consumers, and, second, the development of coherent demands for measures to control the ownership and application of the new technologies. To date, there is little discussion within the labour movement or the consumer movement despite the obvious implications for their constituencies. The people of developing countries have most, potentially, to gain or suffer from new technologies, yet with a host of apparently more pressing matters to address, from debt to climate change, HIV/Aids to world trade talks, it is scarcely surprising the matter is undiscussed in government or civil society.

What follows is a roundup of some of the dangers evident in the development of nanotechnology. As with the sections dealing with potential applications, it is far from complete.

Health and safety: a new asbestos?

It is strong and flexible. It is virtually indestructible. Its heat resistance is phenomenal. It found uses in virtually every type of building as a construction material and as insulation and fireproofing and to alter texture. From floor covering to flower pots, nuclear plants to schools, brake linings to paints, it was an important material. Yet by 1918, US insurance companies were refusing to insure asbestos. Tens of thousands of shipyard workers are estimated to have died as a result of exposure to asbestos. Up to half a million US citizens exposed to asbestos before 1980 may have died from resultant illness with 10,000 still dying each year, according to the Baltimore-based White Lung Association. Figures of a similar order are reported for Europe. The asbestos trade is international, though, with main producers including Russia, Canada, China, Brazil and Zimbabwe and major consumer regions being the Far East, Russia and Kazakhstan, the Middle East, South Asia, and Central and South America. The International Ban Asbestos Secretariat describes the tactics of the industry as similar to those of the tobacco industry, replacing lost sales in developed countries with heavy marketing in developing countries. Incidence of asbestos-related illness in developing countries is forecast to outstrip that in developed countries. In India and South Africa there have been campaigns to have asbestos mining banned and South African workers took Cape plc to court to seek compensation for their suffering. The scale of payouts for asbestos liabilities for a while threatened the survival of huge chunks of the world's insurance business.

The danger posed by asbestos comes from the tiny size of its fibres. These enter the body and cannot be expelled, leading to a range of cancers affecting many different parts of the body. Inhalation into the lung can lead to asbestosis, a scarring of lung tissue that progressively inhibits breathing. Although asbestos-related illnesses are primarily associated with the miners who dig the stuff out and workers who manufacture products from the mineral, there is proven danger from exposure to anyone who comes in contact with the fibres, from firefighters to those who wash workers' clothing, people living near mines and those exposed to asbestos products.

A connection between the proven danger of asbestos fibres and nanoparticles is intuitively obvious if still the subject of expert research. It has already generated an amount of concern, again not least in insurance companies that might have to pick up the bill for compensation claims. A study by Swiss Re called for 'minute scrutiny' of all nanoparticles rather than the current medical re-search concentration on nanotubes.[4] As with asbestos, the potential health effects of nanoparticles are judged to be chronic rather than acute, not manifesting themselves for perhaps years, it notes. If problems emerged only after a long period, 'an unforeseeably large loss potential could accumulate, for example, in the field of health impairment'. Removing the jargon, what that means is that the insurers fear major payouts due to illnesses proved to be caused by nanoparticles. The report goes on to express concern that while it may be possible to assess the risks associated with products with direct access to the body, such as food or medication, 'if the hazard were to spread to the environment, the air and our drinking water, this would not be the case'.[5]

The comparison, whether it proves well-founded or not, between nanotubes or nanoparticles in general and asbestos leaps quickly to mind, but there are a variety of ways in which the integrity of the body can be breached by such minute particles.[6] Airborne particles may be inhaled from paints or sprays or dust whether the contact comes from a product bought from a supermarket or from materials used at work. There are at least four concerns:

1. The particles may inhibit the operation of the lung through irritation and that may be greater the smaller the particles due to their relatively bigger surface area.
2. The substance of nanoparticle size may be a known toxin that can find its way through conventional protection such as face masks due to its size.
3. Some nanoparticles appear to have a catalysing effect that generates free radicals, associated with tumour generation.
4. The substance may exhibit harmful properties at the nanoscale that it does not show at a larger scale, a finding from research into air pollution particles.

Use of nanoparticles in cosmetics and sun lotions has already stimulated concern at Swiss Re, which called it 'imperative' that medical researchers came to agreement on whether they can be absorbed into the blood through the skin.[7] The gut is another possible route of entry, wanted or unwanted, of nanoparticles into the body. The smaller the particles, the more are absorbed and the deeper they penetrate. Much attention has been paid to how and when nanoparticles can cross the blood–brain barrier into the best protected organ of the body.

The surface area effects of nanoscale particles, their catalytic properties, the possibility they may be able to trick the immune system or slip through the defences of the brain or a fetus epitomise the double-edged nature of nanotechnology. It is precisely the properties that cause concern about injury to health of humans (and, indeed, other animals) that excite medical researchers and the shareholders of pharmaceutical companies. The toxicity of water-soluble carbon nanoparticles in some human cells demonstrates a possible means of attacking some cancers and bacterial infections. A pathway through the blood–brain barrier is seen as a route to treating conditions such as Alzheimer's.

It is clear that much more research is needed. Extrapolation of results from experiments on fish or rats is notoriously controversial and, therefore, inadequate. A report on the implications of nanotechnology by Nanoforum, an EU Commission-sponsored network, stated baldly that 'Currently, no one knows if the responses observed in animal experiments would be similar in humans.'[8] But it also notes that 'Some public health studies have found links between engineered nanoparticles and a wide range of health impacts, including, for example, increased asthma hospitalizations, heart diseases, chronic bronchitis and even premature death.'[9]

Absence of regulatory control

Yet regulation tailored to nanotechnology and its products is absent. Although both the potential benefits and the potential risks posed by products based on nanoscience derive from the distinctive characteristics displayed by particles of that size – be it different sensitivity to light, greater surface area, conductive qualities or whatever – regulatory authorities do not take scale into account systematically when assessing new products. The Royal Society report notes with concern that in current EU legislation, nanoparticles of existing chemicals face no additional scrutiny and that up to the time of the report there was no move to treat them as new substances requiring new scrutiny in new regulations under negotiation.[10]

The Food and Drug Administration in the US regulates products representing some 20 per cent of consumer purchases in the domestic market. While the FDA has taken some steps to coordinate its approach to nanotechnology, products using nanoscience may be dealt with by one or more of several departments. The agency's own explanation of its approach highlights laxity in overall FDA policy and in that related to nanotechnology in particular.[11] At the pre-approval stage, typically it is the producer of a product that identifies and assesses risks, which the FDA then reviews. At the next stage, pre-market acceptance, products are often 'copies of similar products'.

The agency states that it has traditionally regulated products with particulates of nanoscale and, while saying new tests will be required as new toxicological risks are identified, argues that 'the existing battery of pharmacotoxicity tests is probably adequate for most nanotechnology products that we will regulate.' 'Particle size is not the issue', it continues, declining to acknowledge the fundamental point that the difference in the characteristics of particles at their nanoscale as opposed to larger scales is precisely what makes them interesting, useful and, perhaps, dangerous. Indeed, 'If the manufacturer makes no nanotechnology claims regarding the manufacture or performance of the product, FDA may be unaware at the time that the product is in the review and approval process that nanotechnology is being employed.' Then, as the document notes, the FDA has only a limited remit over some potentially high-risk products such as cosmetics and has had few resources to assess such products. It concludes: 'Few resources currently exist to assess the risks that would derive to the general population from the wide-scale deployment of nanotechnology products.'

Nanotechnology and food – echoes of GM

The ETC Group's excellent report on nanotechnology and food and agriculture asserts that nowhere in the world as of November 2004 was there regulation governing the entry of nanoscale products into the food chain.[12] Where there is no regulation, of course, there is no labelling and so no consumer choice whether to buy a product made using nanoparticles or not.

With an ever-increasing number of products on the shelves containing nanoscale ingredients, concern has been registered by insurers. The Munich Re paper cited above states: 'Due to lack of product monitoring in the market, the defects which occur during application and use of the product in practice go unrecorded. Consequently, they cannot be passed on to research and development for product optimisation purposes'.[13]

Much of this is familiar. As the ETC paper argued:

> Genetically modified crops came to market less than one decade ago with virtually no public discussion of their risks and benefits, and within regulatory frameworks that civil society organisations have described as inadequate, non-transparent or non-existent. As a result, questions and controversies surrounding socio-economic, health and environmental impacts of GM foods are unresolved and millions of people have spurned GM products. The parallels between the introduction of biotech and nanotech are undeniable. Despite the nanotech community's persistent vows not to repeat the same clumsy mistakes, it has been following in biotech's footsteps.[14]

One of the most important failings of the regulatory authorities in the early days of the biotechnology industry was their lack of expertise in the new science they were charged with overseeing. Jennifer Ferrara documents this in her essay in 'Redesigning Life' where she shows how corporate pressure and US governmental unwillingness to risk being left behind in an important new commercial field through the 1970s and 1980s permitted the research and corporate communities to make the running, asserting that genetic engineering was no more than an extension of traditional crop and animal breeding techniques and that bio-engineered products did not differ fundamentally from non-engineered organisms.[15] So, as long as the genes used come from an already approved food source, the GM product is treated as natural rather than new and requiring special scrutiny. The parallel with the treatment of nanoscale particles in products – including food products – as basically the same as products with larger-scale particles of the same chemicals is obvious.

The scandal of Monsanto's recombinant Bovine Growth Hormone (rBGH) exposed the inability of the Food and Drug Administration to police the new products or to stand up to corporate pressure. Important safety concerns about the effect of the growth hormone on cattle and on humans was hidden and the FDA chose to cover up awkward research rather than admit incompetence. Indeed, the agency's guidelines of February 1994 even took measures to head off potential consumer concerns, saying labelling should state that there was no difference between rBGH and natural hormones. In the US, rBGH milk was pooled with non-rBGH milk in the late 1980s, ensuring that it was impossible to choose to avoid the former (without expending time and energy seeking out organically farmed supplies).[16]

The ballooning growth in the use of Monsanto's Roundup Ready soybeans (modified to resist the company's herbicide) despite concerns about potential spread of the resistance to other plants, possible allergic responses, and generally increased dependence on agro-chemicals, means that no fewer than 30,000 food products, 60 per cent of all processed foods in industrialised countries, could contain genetically modified soybeans.[17]

No more than a handful of food products are currently known to contain nanoparticles, although well over a hundred food industry applications were in development in late 2004, according to the ETC Group.[18] In the case of pesticides and herbicides, the dominant GM players such as Monsanto and Syngenta are in the forefront of nanoscience research and development. They can be expected to exert just as much leverage in ensuring products using nanoparticles, in the delivery of chemicals to crops for instance, are regulated to their advantage as they have with GM products.

Consumer resistance in Europe to GM food delivered a major blow to the biotech industry, leading in the UK, for example, to major supermarket chains telling suppliers they did not wish to stock GM foods.

The US took the EU to the World Trade Organisation's dispute settlement panel in 2003, arguing that it had imposed a five-year moratorium on imports of new varieties of GM food. The EU's defence was that it had simply not approved new varieties while it drew up a new regulatory framework in response to consumer concerns and as a way of restoring confidence in biotechnology. In April 2004, the EU began implementing new legislation on labelling for GM food, feedstuffs and ingredients, legislation deemed to be the strictest in the world and affecting an estimated 90 per cent of GM imports into the EU. The US response was to say its complaint to the WTO would stand because, given the preponderance of GM foodstuffs in the US, the labelling rules were discriminatory and would cost US producers hundreds of millions of dollars a year.

The EU's labelling regime is not watertight but it represents a significant victory for the European consumer. The international implications of the European resistance to US corporate and government pressures were not lost on anyone. The refusal of some African countries to accept GM food as 'aid' was defended by the EU, which stated:

> A number of developing countries, including a large number of African countries suffering a shortage of food, have requested main donors of food aid to avoid providing GMO food. The European Commission finds it unacceptable that such legitimate concerns are used by the US against the EU policy on GMOs. The European Commission believes that it is the legitimate right of developing countries' governments to fix their own level of protection and to take the decision they deem appropriate to prevent unintentional dissemination of GM seeds.
>
> Food aid to starving populations should be about meeting the urgent humanitarian needs of those who are in need. It should not be about trying to advance the case for GM food abroad (while staying away from the international consensus such as the Cartagena Protocol), or planting GM crops for export, or indeed finding outlets for domestic surplus, which is a regrettable [aspect] of the US food aid policy.

One might note in parentheses the irony of such concerns being expressed by an EU that continues to operate a farm subsidy regime that locks out the produce of developing countries. However, the pertinent question here is whether governments and corporations and consumers – individually or collectively – have learned from the GM food experience. Will the EU come under the same consumer pressure over nanotechnology or, at least, some of its more sensitive applications – those with a high 'fright factor' in risk-analysis speak – as it did over GM foods? Will there be a replication of the transatlantic divide over consumer acceptance and labelling policy? If so, can we expect to see new trade disputes, mediated by a WTO that has no agreements specifically related to nanotechnology?

Sue Dibb, senior policy officer of Britain's National Consumer Council (NCC), recognises the danger that nanotechnology could creep up on society, rather as GM foods did, and urges a wide debate over its threats and promises. She also argues that the issue of characteristics of materials changing with scale is clearly vital in evaluating nanoparticle-based products, saying, 'It would be hard to justify an approach that does not recognise there are differences.'[19] Current toxicity testing procedures must be assessed for relevance to nanoscale products.

However, nanotechnology is not a priority for the NCC. Nor is it a priority for the international groupings of consumer organisations even if it is beginning to encroach on their radar screens. In part this is because the remit of many consumer organisations is simply to monitor products on shelves rather than pre-empt possible future problems. Another difficulty is that nanotechnology is a basket of processes and products, current and future, rather than being confined to one or two sectors. That makes it more difficult to track.

Ignorance in the workplace

There is little literature on nanotechnology in the workplace, despite the routinely expressed concerns that nanoparticles might turn out to be the asbestos dust of the twenty-first century. One reason for this is clearly that very few workers are currently exposed to the new technology. This will change as advances in the laboratory are commercialised and enter industrial application. In the car industry alone there is the scope for hundreds of thousands of workers to come into contact with nanoparticles used in bodywork, coatings, catalytic converters or display panels. Estimates from the US envisage 2 million workers dealing with nanotechnology in a handful of years.

The Royal Society report pointed to the health concerns over nanoparticles in the workplace and recommended that the UK Health and Safety Executive (HSE) reduce its occupational exposure limits while it reviews evidence that nanoparticles may be more toxic than their larger cousins. It also called for review of assessment and control of workplace exposure and accidental release procedures. The HSE organised one of the first conferences dedicated to health implications of nanotechnology in late 2004 but remains without a fully developed policy. In early 2005, the government responded by announcing a review of existing regulations but drew immediate criticism for failing to provide funding for requisite research.

The Royal Society took evidence from some 150 organisations as it prepared its report for government. Not one of these was a trade union. To date the response of the labour movement to nanotechnology as a health issue (or any other kind of issue for that matter) has been desultory. The Trades Union Congress, an umbrella for British trade unions, has produced a two-page leaflet on nanotechnology but it contains little information useful to workplace organisers, calling for the rigorous implementation of current regulations, thus missing the point that there may be new threats to address. Even the major international union federation for energy and chemical and mine workers, a strong voice on corporate responsibility issues, has no involvement in research on nanotechnology's implications for workers. The UN's International Labour Organisation is not working on the issue. Rather, it was Swiss Re, with its vested interest in not footing the bill for a new wave of industrial injury compensation payments, which stated:

In view of the dangers to society that could arise out of the establishment of nanotechnology, and given the uncertainty currently
prevailing in scientific circles, the precautionary principle should
be applied whatever the difficulties. The handling of nanotechno
logically manufactured substances should be carefully assessed and
accompanied by appropriate protective measures. This is particularly
important for individuals whose jobs expose them to nanoparticles
on a regular basis.[20]

Nanoparticles in our earth, air and water

If nanoparticles pose questions of health for producers and consumers, it is evident that their release, controlled or uncontrolled,
poses wider environmental questions. What happens when a factory
releases waste slurry of nanoparticles into a river, or a landfill site
takes in truckloads of domestic and industrial nano-waste, or there
is an explosion at a plant making nanotubes? Again, the insurance
industry has been quick to worry about the consequences to its
profit margins. The Munich Re report cited earlier notes:

> The manufacture of nanotechnology products will aggravate the
> conventional risks of third party losses and damage to natural re-
> sources. Not only people, property and capital but also the environ-
> mental constituents of earth, air and water are threatened by losses
> in any number of: laboratories; manufacturing plants; warehouses;
> waste management and waste disposal plants; outdoor trial areas; as
> well as by damage caused by the products themselves.[21]

The report of the EU-funded Nanoforum on the benefits and
risks of nanotechnology cites four routes by which nanoparticles
could infiltrate the environment: dispersal in their manufactured
form, adsorbtion with other substances, aggregation and uptake
by cells. As with the direct impact on human health, there is little
established knowledge. As the report puts it:

little is known about the fate, transport, and transformation of nanosized particles after they enter the environment. Nobody knows if they are toxic or not today, or if they could be toxic within months or years. So, these nano-elements could be non-biodegradable pollutants.[22]

There are already concerns being expressed by researchers over the impact on soil ecology of titanium dioxide nanoparticles that appear to burn up bacteria, while buckyballs perform in un-expected ways when inserted into the ground.

The large surface areas, exchange capacity and strong electrical charges of nanoparticles suggests they would tend to bind with other substances in the environment. The concern, Nanoforum points out, is that they bind with toxins. Colloids – suspensions of nanoparticles in other substances – are renowned for their ability to hold and transport pollutants. Released into water systems, toxic colloids could travel quickly and be difficult to trace.

Work done to date shows a tendency of nanoparticles in lakes and acquifers to aggregate with other particles. This may limit the distance they travel, which could be a good thing, but it is also possible that they aggregate with toxic particles and form a new toxic conglomerate.

Biotic uptake is the incorporation of a substance by a living tissue, and it clearly threatens to introduce that substance into the food chain. The Nanoforum report lists a catalogue of hugely damaging industrial processes involving biotic uptake, including the solvents released by the semiconductor industry, synthetic chemicals such as DDT and Freon, and the use of natural com-pounds asbestos and chlorine.[23]

Nanotechnology is already being used by the giant agrochemical groups in pesticides. As time progresses, it will enable them to produce finely tuned release systems, delivering precise quantities of chemicals and releasing them only in specific circumstances such as the presence or absence of water or at particular pH levels or when given a particular sonic, optical or magnetic signal. This is the agricultural application of the promises that so tantalise medical researchers. But it is also likely to raise concerns familiar from the GM food debacle about the deliberate introduction of new substances into the food chain and into the wider environment.

Some mention should be made at this point of the one nanotechnology scare that has excited some popular and press interest. Through the agency of popular film and fiction and the concerns voiced for many years by Eric Drexler, and latterly by the heir to the British throne, the fear of 'grey goo' has overshadowed other more pressing questions about the implications of nanotechnology. The frightening if hypothetical danger of self-replicating nanobots running amok is the ultimate environmental threat. It is also, as the ETC Group has pointed out, a nightmare for commercial interests, which have not addressed more immediate concerns over nanotechnology and which fear a public backlash such as that which has slowed commercialisation of GM foods.

'Grey goo' refers to what would notionally be left of the world in the wake of 'global ecophagy', a consequence of the runaway self-replication of nanobots. Drexler envisaged an exponential growth in the number of such self-replicators of such speed and magnitude that it would consume everything in its wake, literally destroying the world. As the vision of what is now politely called 'advanced nanotechnology' and less politely belittled as the ramblings of scaremongers is sidelined in the interests of shorter-term commercial gain, so concerns over self-replication are being put back in the cupboard. In fact, Drexler himself has moved to calm the fears he articulated two decades ago. His early conceptualisation of molecular manufacturing was based on a biological model of self-replicating nanobots. Now he says, 'Molecular machine systems can be thoroughly non-biological, and self-replication in not necessary'.[24] The model he has now adopted is, conceptually, little different from an automated factory of today but at the nanoscale with small parts assembled to make larger ones by conveyor belts and assembly robots. Any single component, if removed from the system, 'would be as inert as a light bulb pulled from its socket'.

However, while the grey goo scare may have little foundation at present, it would be ill advised to forget it entirely. There are two reasons for this. First, it stands as a cipher for less apocalyptic but nonetheless extreme dangers that might accompany the escape of highly reactive and little understood agents into the soil, air or water – nanoparticles need not be biological or self-replicating to set off chain reactions. Second, not only is nanotechnology a basket of technologies melding a basket of disciplines, it is itself within a basket of emerging technologies that includes genetic engineering and artificial intelligence. With the increasing interaction of these emerging technologies, the divisions between the 'natural' and the 'artificial', the organic and inorganic, the biological and non-biological are crumbling. Working at the molecular scale, the distinctions are decreasingly relevant. Marrying biotechnology and nanotechnology is already well under way. For example, at the University of California in Los Angeles, rat heart cells have been attached to plastic or silicon-based artificial muscles to create tiny robots that grow, multiply and assemble – that are, as their developer said, 'alive'.[25]

Remediation: out of the frying pan into the fire?

While the concerns mentioned so far derive from accidental or at least incidental introduction of nanoparticles into the wider environment, an important area to consider is the deliberate use of nanoscience with the intention of repairing the environment.

Mention has already been made of paints and coatings capable of absorbing airborne pollutants, mitigating the effects of vehicle exhaust in town centres. The exterior walls of the Shanghai World Expo pavilions were to be coated with a nanoparticle paint that would then be used on public building in the city and, potentially, on road surfaces.[26] Self-organising carpets of nanotubes have proved capable of killing bacteria and might be developed further into tools for identifying and neutralising a variety of chemical and biological agents.

The Environmental Protection Agency in the US provides seed funding for a number of projects aimed at using nanotechnology to identify and remedy environmental threats. These include filters to remove arsenic from drinking water and air pollutant sensors. In 1980 the US government established the Superfund, a programme to clean up sites worst affected by chemical pollution. In 2004 alone the Superfund spent $507 million on site clean-up work and secured commitments of $680 million from parties responsible for the degradation. The programme has some 1,500 sites on its clean-up list. On top of this, there are estimated to be 150,000 underground storage sites awaiting decontamination. The cost of cleaning up sites contaminated by the US defence department's use of the solvent trichloroethene alone is estimated at $5 billion.

Clearly the historic and future costs of cleaning up after industry are vast even in developed countries with a long, if inadequate, history of regulation of manufacturing industry and industrial farming. In industrialising countries there is the risk of corners being cut in the name of rapid economic growth and because corporations from the developed world are as happy to take advantage of lax environmental regulation in developing countries as they are to exploit those countries' cheap labour.

Nanoparticles appear to offer a cheap and rapid method of environmental remediation. Nanoscale iron particles have a large surface area and high surface reactivity. They have been shown to be effective at transforming a range of common contaminants, including chlorinated organic solvents, organochlorine pesticides, and polychlorinated biphenyls (used in the past as coolants and lubricants in electrical equipment and associated with skin conditions, cancers and behavioural problems in children). They can be deployed in soil, water or gaseous streams. Nanoparticles of gold and palladium show great promise as catalysts for remediation of trichloroethene. A 2003 academic overview said iron nanoparticle slurries also had potential applications for immobilising the heavy metals and radionuclides such as uranium that pollute some drinking water, sometimes from natural sources but sometimes from pollution from industrial plants producing radioactive material.[27]

The paper documents a field trial where iron nanoparticle slurry containing 11.2 kg of nanoparticles was introduced into groundwater through an injection well over a period of two days. A reduction of over 90 per cent of chlorinated volatile organic compounds was achieved and other pollutants reduced to levels that brought the groundwater to required quality standards, apparently without increasing the concentration of vinyl chlorides.

On the face of it, this is unalloyed good news. Environmental remediation using nanotechnology can help us to repair some of the damage industry and consumerism have done to our health and our environment. But caution is needed. Two issues arise.

The first is what the side effects are of deploying nanoparticles in the environment. This returns us to the open questions about the ability of nanoparticles to penetrate living organisms and their impact when they have done so. Chemists standardly address whether the chemical transformations achieved through decontamination create daughter products that might be harmful in themselves. However, when nanoscale particles are introduced into the soil or groundwater they are being inserted at the very bottom of the food chain. Without full knowledge of their toxicity throughout that chain, this would be a dangerous enterprise. Nonetheless, in principle, this issue can be resolved empirically.

The second issue is cultural, and links in with other questions of how nanotechnology and other new technologies change our relationship with the world around us. Rampant capitalism has transformed labour into a commodity. The products of labour, be they automobiles or works of literature, sacks of wheat or television dramas, are reduced to the status of commodity. The environment is reduced to the status of a repository of the raw materials needed for commodity production and the receiver of the waste products of the production and consumption of those commodities. The results are the deadly pollution of Bhopal in India or Timisoara in Romania, the blighted landscapes of open-cast mining, the destruction of the ozone layer, massive increases in respiratory and skin diseases, fisheries on the verge of extinction, and global warming that is set vastly to increase the incidence of war, famine, migration and 'natural' disasters. The islands on the planet not directly affected by the throwaway culture of the commodity are those over which the tide of capital has yet to flow fully and, ironically, those whose value as commodities in themselves outweighs their value as sources of commodities or refuse dumps, namely tourist destinations from Tuscany to the Masai Mara to Bondai Beach.

As the consequences of such vast and perhaps irreversible destruction sink in – even in the Pentagon, if not the White House – there is a danger that nanotechnology (and other new technologies) will provide succour to those who seek to address only (some of) the results of this way of life rather than its causes. The opportunities for environmental remediation that nanotechnology may offer are likely to be seized upon by those who prefer to maintain fossil fuel use and the inexorable tide of global warming while applying the sticking plaster of lower particulate levels in city centres, courtesy of the latest nano-surfacing.

Of course, we should adopt technologies and products that mitigate the symptoms of an increasingly devastated environment. But while the vested interests use any new technology to defend their sunk investments, the rest of us need to beware a cultural shift towards viewing the environment as remediable or replaceable, for that leads either to acceptance of unsustainable production and consumption patterns or to the dangerous illusion that creeps in to some nanotechnology visions of removing ourselves to other planets.

6

From Cold War to Star Wars
to Nanowars?

In the Cold War (and since), rough geo-strategic parity was achieved and maintained by the balance of terror known as the doctrine of mutually assured destruction. Each side knew the other would have time and ability to wreak havoc on its opponent in the event of an attack. President Reagan's 'Star Wars' initiative was dangerous because it sought to undermine the doctrine by depriving the Soviet Union of the assurance it could destroy the US if Washington chanced a first strike.

The danger with the emerging technologies, Gubrud argues (along with others), is that while none of the diverse government, academic or commercial research programmes looks close to realising anything as revolutionary as self-replicating assemblers and their theoretical potential to exceed the neutron bomb in selective destruction, at the point when it becomes clear that such a breakthrough is possible within, say, five years, a race will be inevitable:

> Industry will be heavily involved, but national efforts will be stimulated and coordinated by government and military initiatives. The leading competitors will be those with the greatest concentration of advanced technology: the United States, Japan and Europe.

However, the race will also be joined by countries such as Russia, China, India, Israel and others that have a strong technology base, a lot of resources, or both.[1]

In the event of one country or military bloc gaining a significant advantage, it would confront the decision whether or not to impose its desired world order before others caught up. If, on the other hand, the race proved relatively equal with an advance in one key area in one place matched by another somewhere else, the consequence would be a spiralling competition with each party striving to keep up with and decisively overtake the others quantitatively and qualitatively. Moreover, would fear of being left far behind in the new arms race tempt those with nuclear or chemical arsenals to wield them while they still had value?

Just as wider access to information and technical expertise led to fears of nuclear or biological weapons proliferation among not only states but also non-state players, be they 'reds under the bed' or 'Islamic extremists', so increasing attention is being paid to the possibility of nanoweapon proliferation beyond the major powers. If nanoscience products and processes are to become widespread across industries, to some extent they must become 'off-the-shelf' packages, easily and relatively cheaply available. And let us not forget that if nanoparticles do have the capacity to debilitate health or efficiently transport infections, there will be the potential for the development of nano-equivalents of the nuclear 'dirty bomb' – low-technology delivery of a relatively inefficient, unsophisticated but nonetheless deadly payload, delivering fibres into the lungs or illness into the bloodstream rather than exposure to radiation.

So, the UK Ministry of Defence worries:

Manipulation of biological and chemical species using nanotechnology techniques could result in new threats that might be hard to detect and counter. Terrorist and non-governmental organisation groups might attack elements of the national infrastructure, for example by some form of non-traceable activity affecting crops or animal livestock.[2]

The same thinking is found in the US, where the defence review cited earlier[3] notes the rapid advance in military technologies: 'This poses the danger that states hostile to the United States could significantly enhance their capabilities by integrating widely available off-the-shelf technologies into their weapons systems and armed forces.' Further on it notes that the US has been surprised by the speed at which other states have developed weapons of mass destruction and how rapidly potential or actual adversaries will acquire new-generation armaments. That uncertainty is, arguably, more likely to provoke pre-emptive action than caution on the part of a neurotic and unpopular superpower.

In 2003, Iraq was invaded on the pretext that its government possessed weapons of mass destruction. The motor of US foreign policy under George W. Bush has been the demonising of states deemed inimical to the US. A frequent allegation – whether as ill founded as that against the former Iraqi dictatorship or not – has been their development of weapons of mass destruction. The weaponry concerned has been nuclear and chemical, both of which require relatively large and easy-to-identify fabrication facilities and delivery systems. Conceptually at any rate, advanced nanoweaponry would not need the scale of plant, thus increasing the potential for baseless charges to be levelled at other states and removing the embarrassment of being unable to locate evidence.

The development of sensors and much-enhanced remotely controlled vehicles, let alone offensive nanobots, extends the push towards war at arm's length by technologically advanced armies. Missile technology and bomb guidance systems have long permitted the military to stand back from the scene of slaughter, to destroy without serious risk to its own personnel. On a battlefield where evenly matched opponents were pitted, one can almost imagine a bloodless contest for territorial advantage. And herein lies danger. Technology turns war into a computer game, with screen representations mediating between target and attacker. With weaponry of increased precision operated from a distance by men reacting to data from computer screens, the enemy is dehumanised perhaps more effectively than through traditional propaganda.

The ultimate distance from the enemy and 'survivable' conflict might be achieved by war conducted from, via or in space. US programmes to militarise space, from those of Reagan to those of Bush, have committed vast sums of money for little concrete return in terms of deployed weaponry (although there have been geopolitical consequences). A paper by the Organisation for Economic Cooperation and Development listed twelve major contributions nanotechnology will bring to space architectures, from lightweight reusable launch vehicles to autonomous spacecraft and micro-craft.[4] There can be no doubt that the military will be the first to seize upon such developments.

Intermediation and distance both dehumanise the consequences of conflict for those who deploy advanced weaponry and encourage the notion that large-scale war is survivable. Along with allied technological trends, particularly development of artificial intelligence, nanotechnology can only exacerbate this danger. Manuel De Landa in his book *War in the Age of the Intelligent Machines*, written after the 1991 war against Iraq, draws attention to a further shift:

> For now, the robot simply makes the job of its human remote-controller easier by preprocessing some the information itself, or even by making and then relaying a preliminary assessment of events within its visual field.
>
> But it is precisely the distinction between advisory and executive capabilities that is being blurred in other military applications of artificial intelligence.[5]

He goes on to describe how automata have encroached on and then replaced humans in military war gaming. Human participants were found to be unwilling to cross the nuclear threshold in training exercises so computers were put in their place.

> To the extent that the 'insights' derived from watching automata fight simulated armageddons actually find their way into strategic doctrine and contingency plans, these 'robot events' have already begun to blur the distinction between a purely advisory and an executive role for intelligent machines.

Of course, powerful and technologically advanced nations have not faced up against each other – except by proxy – since the Second World War. There is no battle of equals. There is Mutla Ridge, which stands for all the turkey-shoots of the two recent wars against Iraq. There is the mis-guided ordnance that takes out bomb shelters in Baghdad and the list of wedding parties bombed in Afghanistan and Iraq.

The technological divide may be much narrower when soldiers are deployed on the ground but it remains wide. Insurgents may be able to inflict casualties on modern armies, but body armour and high-tech reconnaissance render those casualties fewer and lighter. The Future Force Warrior programme described earlier, with its objective of a Robocop-style fighter, represents another conceptual blurring between soldier and machine. He is fully wired, armoured, has superhuman strength, the most up-to-date weaponry and self-medication. Does his invulnerability and consequently lower body-bag count increase the acceptability of conflict and overseas adventurism? Is it qualitatively different from past technological divides in weaponry: the longbow over the mounted knight; the rifle over the musket; the tank over infantry?

The Center for Responsible Nanotechnology[6] has pointed out a further danger posed by the militarisation of nanoscience.

If civilian access to molecular manufacturing threatens illicit generation of weapons of mass destruction (or even proliferation of dual-use technology), then the state is likely to establish firm control over the processes, keeping them closely guarded. If that is the case, the opportunities for access for purposes beneficial to the public even in the developed world, let alone in developing countries considered unreliable by the powerful government, will be very much reduced.

The enemy within

Public acceptance of high levels of military spending or military action abroad, whether during the Cold War or the 'War against Terror', is facilitated by the search for the 'enemy within', real or imaginary. McCarthyite witch-hunts or the harassment of Muslim communities or the search for the al-Qaeda sleepers who 'could be attending Christian worship services on Sunday mornings',[7] keep neighbour watching neighbour while justifying the development of new government agencies, the passage of laws restricting civil liberties, and the employment of technology against the public.

Winston in *Nineteen Eighty-four* struggled through a life where surveillance had reached a degree that Orwell pitched as conceivable enough to provoke thought but verging on science fiction:

> In the far distance a helicopter skimmed down between the roofs, hovered for an instant like a bluebottle, and darted away again with a curving flight. It was the police patrol, snooping into people's windows...
>
> Behind Winston's back the voice from the telescreen was still babbling away ... The telescreen received and transmitted simultaneously. Any sound that Winston made, above the level of a very low whisper, would be picked up by it, moreover, so long as he remained within the field of vision which the metal plaque commanded, he

could be seen as well as heard. ... You had to live – did live, from habit that became instinct – in the assumption that every sound you made was overheard, and, except in darkness, every movement scrutinized.[8]

Twenty years after the titular date of Orwell's dystopian vision, there is no street in the City of London that is not surveyed by closed-circuit television cameras. Political activists and civil rights campaigners in the most far-flung parts of the world swap around mobile phones and SIM cards because they know the authorities can and do monitor not just calls but locations of callers. Iris recognition software is about to become standard, life mimicking the Hollywood film where every individual's location can be monitored by scanners and the only way of avoiding recognition is by an eye transplant.

Nanotechnology's potential massively to enhance sensing and monitoring capability is a prime example of the way scientific advance offers both vast improvement in lives and their degradation, control and destruction. The use to which technology is put is a question of economic and political control of that technology.

It is commonly said that nanotechnology will soon provide sensors and mini-computers woven into clothing or dotted around the house to monitor the health of the elderly or check that a balanced diet is being followed.

For the whole product chain from supply sourcing through manufacture, transport, retail and after-sales care, the placing of minute sensors on anything from a carton of milk to an aircraft offers the possibility of better control. Inputs or finished products could be monitored for degradation. Location could be checked for every item, far exceeding the control of stocks and deliveries delivered by a transponder on a lorry or shipping container. Food products could warn when they had passed their sell-by date by a change in colour of the packaging. A service contract could include provision of equipment-monitoring sensors that would warn consumer and contractor alike when an item needed attention.

Yet put this technology in the hands of security services and they will have powers that make those of Orwell's Big Brother pale and make the reach of Romania's former Securitate into individual, family and workplace life seem trivial. Intelligence, whether gathered by security services or by corporations, depends to a large and increasing extent on the profiling of populations, the matching of characteristics with activities, tendencies, predilictions. Access to credit-card transactions, telephone records, survey results, information gleaned from 'data miners' implanted via the Internet, already allows individuals and communities to be profiled, tracked and sorted. The all-pervasive sensor technology that is now envisaged poses an enormous threat to civil liberties.

The volume of electronic data transmission already presents problems for the security apparatus. The exponential growth of such traffic means the problem of monitoring and storage also grows in leaps and bounds. At present in the European Union countries it is entirely in the hands of national governments what access to communications data they give to their agencies. In the UK, for example, communications data can be accessed without a warrant on grounds of security or prevention of crime. This data is not the content of a telephone call – that does require judicial endorsement. It is unclear whether it includes the URL of a website visited. But it does enable a lot of information to be collected, including identities, addresses and phone numbers of callers and recipients, timing and duration of call, location, use of facilities such as voice messaging or encryption.

Whether such data is only collected on individuals known to be about to commit the most heinous of crimes or on whole communities is a question of political choice and control over the security apparatus but there are also technical parameters defined by collection, storage and access capacity. However, these parameters would be blown away by the massive leaps in computing that are being developed as the industry begins the shift from the micro- to the nanoscale. Previously unfeasible volumes of data will be able to be stored and faster computers will enable it to be sorted and accessed with ease. The parallelism envisaged for future quantum or bio-molecular computers will enable decryption not just of coding used by real or imagined conspirators but also that used by anyone who sends encrypted messages from home or work, as millions do every day.

7

The great divide

A Parisian boulevard, the Eiffel Tower in the middle distance and a corner café in the foreground. The Tower is now coated with super-efficient anti-corrosion paint. The window panes of the café are of thermochromic glass that regulates the influx of light. A customer works on a laptop computer with compact data memory based on the magnetic 'spin' of electrons. A personal assistant in his pocket is self-powered and will do everything from act as a television screen to translate instructions to the waiter. Another customer rests her new, bio-compatible hip joints and watches a cyclist speed by. His bicycle is light as a feather, his clothing reads his pulse and respiration. The car behind him glides quietly along, powered by fuel cells with scarcely a vibration as piezo mats counter surface bumps. The street is pleasant to sit out in because there is no longer the stink of petrol and diesel fumes. Service is rapid because the order can be given and paid for electronically.

Across the Mediterranean and over the Sahara, somewhere in the Sahel, lies a village. As darkness approaches, light emanates from the houses as solar power systems gathering energy from matting on the roofs and walls release electricity to each household. At the standpumps there is less concern than there used to be about the quality of drinking water because it is now run quickly and effectively through cheap, small and long-lasting filters. There is still plenty of illness in the village, especially among the children and the elderly, of whom there seem to be more these days, but diagnosis is so much quicker than it used to be. It is not that there are more doctors or nurses in town but that when a paramedic arrives in the village, she can do so much more. With a gadget that fits in her hand she can get through the population of the school in a day, checking every child for a range of illnesses. A number of conditions, including HIV/Aids and malaria, are being spotted early now so treatment can be considered. The school used to get by with a single teacher trained decades ago and using books often written before the children's parents were born. Now, the children sit in front of a large screen for much of the day, receiving lessons from the ether while the teacher, retrained through distance learning, deals with individual pupils. It is said that the school library is now the size of a matchbox yet contains every book in the biggest of Africa's libraries. The village continues to depend for food primarily on its livestock and a limited amount of agriculture. The incessant march of climate change reduces rainfall year by year; once semi-fertile land is now a dustbowl. But the crops are holding out better than expected now that they are fed with a new range of chemicals that releases nutrients just when they are needed. Sensors mean that stray animals are easier to locate and their owners know when a prize beast is sickening and can consider whether it is worth treating.

The first tableau is found in a European Commission document explaining nanotechnology to the general public.[1] The street and its population are clean and prosperous (and white). The scene lacks realism in that it is uncrowded but otherwise demands little stretch of the imagination to believe it to be a representation of a

Paris of a generation from now. The second tableau is not to be found in the document. But the potential benefits of advances in energy provision, water filtering, medical diagnostics, communication and food science for the developing world, particularly its rural regions, are clear, indeed much starker than they are for the wealthy inhabitants of a Western European consumer society.

Yet to find the second tableau credible requires not a gentle flexing of the imagination but a giant leap because the distribution of the benefits of technology is determined not by need but by political and economic muscle.

The UN Development Programme's *Human Development Report 2003* estimated more than 1 billion people live in extreme poverty and for many living standards are worsening. The International Energy Agency calculates that some 1.6 billion people have no access to electricity and 2.4 billion rely on traditional biomass sources for fuel. WaterAid estimates that 1.1 billion lack access to safe drinking water with 2 million a year dying as a result. In 2003, 800 million people lacked reliable access to the food they needed to sustain them.

The UNDP administrator said the 2003 *Report* 'shows that there are many countries where income levels are high enough to end absolute poverty, but where pockets of deep poverty remain, often because of worrying patterns of discrimination in the provision of basic services'.[2] The data show patterns of discrimination in access to education, health care, safe water and sanitation, with the rural poor, women and ethnic minorities taking the brunt. The patterns of poverty are self-replicating as well. Distance from drinking water directly correlates to the proportion of girls attending school, for example. Use of biomass is often linked to respiratory illnesses, lower agricultural yields, environmental degradation and, again, low school attendance by girls (who are expected to collect the fuel). But political will can break the vicious circle. China was

providing 98 per cent of its population with at least a rudimentary
electricity supply in 2002, although 56 per cent were still defined
as poor – living on less than $2 a day (as did 2.8 billion people
worldwide in that year).[3]

The benefits of nanotechnology for the developing world are
already trumpeted and will be all the more so as companies and
governments seek to neutralise sceptics, critics and those who
would institute firm regulation. We have, after all, been here
before.

Agriculture

Genetically modified food was and is touted as a solution to
world hunger but the arguments for it have now been thoroughly
debunked, and the reasons for its promotion by the US government in particular and by the four 'gene giant' corporations that
dominate the GM crop market have been exposed.

In a presentation entitled 'Genetically Modified Organisms
Will Not Solve African Hunger', Amadou Kanoute of Consumers
International argued that US provision of GM cereals to African
countries as food aid, as well as limited donation of patent rights,
have been intended to shift an oversupply of GM crops that face
mass consumer rejection, and as a tool to develop new markets.
Adoption of GM crops will not address the political, environmental
and trade-related causes of hunger in Africa but rather will destroy
traditional production models, promote monoculture and eliminate
competition from crops other than the GM varieties controlled
by the 'gene giants'.[4] On the other side of the globe, startling if
fiercely contested evidence has been published suggesting that far
from improving food provision, the massive take-up of GM soya
in Argentina has been a major factor in a crisis that threatens to
engulf the agricultural sector.[5]

Nanoscience will not run parallel with genetic engineering but, rather, the two will be wholly intertwined as the same corporations that dominate the agricultural 'life science' sector today extend that dominance into the delivery systems, sensing, crop monitoring, policing of farmers and food modification that nanotechnology will offer. As the ETC Group put it:

> Agro-nano connects the dots in the industrial food chain and goes one step further down. With new nanoscale techniques of mixing and harvesting genes, genetically modified plants become atomically modified plants. Pesticides can be more precisely packaged to knock out unwanted pests, and artificial flavourings and natural nutrients engineered to please the palate. Visions of an automated, centrally-controlled industrial agriculture can now be implemented using molecular sensors, molecular delivery systems and low-cost labour.[6]

While the low-cost labour of the developing world, whether *in situ* or imported into the polytunnels of southern Europe, may be needed, the small-scale farming of much of Africa and Asia will have no place of importance in the plans of the corporations that will control nanoscience-enhanced agriculture. Nanotechnology's role in agriculture will not be to extend the life expectancy of the family cow or increase the productivity of a cassava patch. It will be to extend further the industrialisation of agriculture with attendant social and environmental consequences.

Information technology

In the context of access to information technology the widening gulf between the haves and the have-nots was named 'the digital divide'. Sales of personal computers worldwide are massive and their penetration into new markets is rapid. A survey in thirty

Chinese cities found the proportion owning computers rose from 17 per cent in 2000 to 30 per cent three years later.[7] But this is an urban phenomenon. Access to computers and Internet usage is determined primarily by income and infrastructure availability (although a number of other factors, including education and regulation, are important). In the US in 2001 there were over 61 computers per hundred head of population against 0.5 in south Asia and 1 in sub-Saharan Africa. Looking at the extremes of the distribution graph, computer penetration in the US was 550 times that of Ethiopia.[8] India's computer ownership rate more recently was 0.9 per cent against a global average of 2.7 per cent.

Within developing countries, very wide disparities in access to technology between those with regular income living in cities and those living in outlying rural areas are scarcely surprising but it was the class and race disparities within the US that first attracted the attention of some academics to the digital divide.

Rural–urban migration and industrialisation are providing vast new markets for information technology manufacturers. Personal computer ownership is forecast to double between 2004 and 2010 with China, India and Russia the driving forces. Low-price local brands are likely to dominate. But even assuming some trickle-down effect, the impact on rural areas and on the urban poor will be minimal and social disparities will be further exacerbated.

The digital divide stands as a cipher for a broader technology divide, ranging from access or lack of access to electricity and basic medicine through to the benefits (and disbenefits) of emerging technologies, including nanotechnology. The RAND report echoes many others when it notes that 'concerns and tensions' already exist and will grow in many countries over the new class disparities that developments in nanotechnology and biotechnology may bring within and between countries.[9] While the odds are that the Parisian street scene will soon become a reality, it would require fundamental changes in the ownership and control of technology before the tableau of the Sahelian village would seem likely to be realised. More likely, perhaps, is a village further depopulated as the land supports less and less farming and the young make their way to cities that seem ever more alien. In just a few years time, the elderly in Europe and North America – certainly the well-heeled among them – will have access to lightweight, very strong replacement hips grown from material compatible with bone; their clothes will monitor their pulse, blood pressure, sugar level, enabling preventive action should one indicator go awry. Diagnosis of serious ailments will be carried out without the need for a hospital visit. Sensors will warn the forgetful that the milk is beyond its use-by date. Meanwhile, in the least developed countries, will life expectancy still be little more than fifty years?

Trade, industry and global employment

The introduction of new technologies frequently brings with it shifts in demand for raw materials. Think of the explosion of demand for oil a century ago or the number of products now made of plastic that were formerly made of metal, or the rise and collapse of the phosphate market in the 1970s. Nanotechnology threatens existing commodity trade patterns between the developing and industrialised worlds. One of the studies by Nanoforum pointed out:

> Furthermore, many developing countries rely on natural resources such as metals, minerals and oil for much of their income. Nano-technology offers the potential to reduce dependency on these resources or even circumvent their use entirely. While this may have advantages for the environment and, in the long term, costs, what is considered less is the effect this decreased dependency will have on the economies of these developing countries. Many a cynic

might look and suggest that the West is removing its dependency on resources that it lacks, and that this is the driving force behind much of these advances.[10]

The ETC Group has highlighted cotton and rubber production as possible casualties of nanoscale materials. In the case of cotton, large-scale marketing of nanotechnologies could well bring a further downward spiral for a commodity that has long been suffering competition from artificial fibres. Patented nanotechnologies alter synthetic fibres so that they reproduce the qualities and texture of cotton. Manufacturers have long used carbon black to strengthen tyres. Indeed carbon black is one of the 'accidental' nanomaterials that has been in use longest. Tyre makers are researching engineered nanomaterials to extend further the life of their products, reducing the demand for rubber, which even in the age of artificial rubber and plastics, still accounts for 50 per cent of a tyre. Work is also going on to develop aerogel tyres that use no rubber at all but comprise nano-air particles in a silica matrix.[11]

Platinum is a relatively rare and highly expensive metal – some $220,000 a kilogram in early 2005. Over 70 per cent of global production is in South Africa. Demand has risen sharply over the last thirty years, much of the growth accounted for by use in catalytic converters that reduce vehicle emissions. Patents have been granted and investors found for nanocomposites that promise to reduce greatly the amount of platinum used in catalytic converters and then replace platinum entirely.

At the same time, increases in scale of production of nanoscale nickel particles threaten to edge platinum out of other roles as a catalyst. For example, it could be replaced in the nascent fuel cell market. Nanoscale nickel particles can be produced for a quarter of the price of platinum and can be used not only as a catalyst but also in the various parts of the cell membrane that currently require a range of different materials.[12]

If, as seems inevitable, carbon nanotube production is stepped up in coming years and begins to find wide employment in composites, strengthening and lightening the bodywork of airplanes and cars for example, there will be a knock-on effect on demand patterns for a range of established materials.

To forecast the impact on commodity markets of newly developed materials, let alone those still at the laboratory research stage, is simply not possible. There are too many variables. For example, if Chinese demand for steel continued to soar it would likely outweigh the impact of reductions in the amount of steel used per car due to use of carbon nanotubes in panels for the foreseeable future. That said, as China has ramped up domestic production of steel to replace imports, it might produce a doubly reduced demand growth in some producer countries. But, of course, demand for cars is growing worldwide, sucking in more and more steel.

Then there is always the issue of whether new materials actually live up to their promise. Artificial rubber made massive inroads into the market for natural rubber but has not replaced it. Similarly, artificial substitutes have not spelled the demise of cocoa or vanilla, however poor markets may have been for producers.

Every significant rise in the price of oil is accompanied by consumer-country programmes to accelerate development of alternative energy forms and improve energy efficiency (as well as demands to use diplomatic or even military means to influence the market), yet forecasts show demand continuing to grow for decades to come.

Nonetheless, however complex the equations, it is very likely that the encroachment of nanotechnology will bring changes in demand patterns for a wide range of raw materials. With the high dependency of many developing countries on raw material exports, this must be a cause for concern that demands economic modelling and political preparedness. To take two commodities referred to earlier, natural rubber is harvested by 30 million farmers in the developing world and 100 million farmers grow cotton. The effect of new technologies and materials on their livelihoods must be a cause for concern.

Primary expressions of reduced demand for raw materials are in employment and workers' income. Lower demand and lower prices for agricultural commodities drive peasant farmers from the land, leaving the way for larger farmers with economies of scale. In mining and industrial farming the result of lower demand and prices is layoffs and further reductions in the purchase workers have over employers.

For decades at the very least the notion of a world where the worker is no longer needed has accompanied technological development. Machinery has changed the workplace for many industrial workers and, indeed, rendered many redundant as factories have become more and more automated and early-nineteenth-century punch-card programmes for looms have been succeeded by powerful computing that directs production. Even skilled engineering, design and fault-detection functions are standardly performed by computers.

Will the development of nanotechnology as process rather than material produce similarly large changes in the structure of industrial work, globally? Here, again, we enter the realm of speculation rather than forecasting. For the visionaries (as noted in an earlier chapter) there is the prospect of a world without workers where everything from food for the table to battleships is built by industrious nanobots supplied with nothing but the chemical constituents of the end product. The fabrication units would be so cheap and portable they could be located anyway, doing away with the need for long distribution chains, replacing trade in raw material and goods.

Should nanoscale assemblers prove practicable, there are two paths down which early models might go. Prototypes and early models might well be massively expensive and very limited in their application, employable only for very specific, precise work for niche markets. On the other hand, a breakthrough on costs might mean a relatively limited range of functions would permit application manufacturing simple products, such as small-scale water pipes. Assuming development continued apace, the latter path would allow nanoscale manufacturing to become a 'disruptive technology' in the original sense of the term, which is of a lower performance, lower-price product that is able to gain a toehold in a market by satisfying customers with needs below those of the technical content and price of incumbent technology. As the new technology improves it squeezes the incumbent out of more and more market segments, eventually replacing it entirely. Christensen's theory of disruptive technology is contested and is only one of a range of theories of technological replacement but it serves to indicate one possible route for nanoscale manufacturing.

Leaving the visions to the visionaries (remembering perhaps that the promises of the 1960s of an end to domestic labour produced microwave ovens, freezers and an array of washing powders but not the robots that were to do the housework), one industry where self-organisation of nanoparticles, on the one hand, and nanoscale fabrication tools, on the other, are most likely to be harnessed in the foreseeable future is electronics. In that industry there is the economic and technical incentive imposed by Moore's laws to use nanotechnology to extend the life of silicon-based architecture and, perhaps, to supersede it. Research into the use of nanotubes in electronics is widespread and able to draw on funding from industry and government. One recent industry study said that examples of guided self-assembly whereby nano-particles would copy a template structure would be available by around 2007.[13] Initially, the forms of self-assembly would be basic, such as forming a molecular layer on the substrate on which the component is based.

The ability to industrialise the use of expensive laboratory tools will be crucial to shifting further down into the nanoscale in the electronics industry. Dip pen nanolithography is a case in point. The technology has been compared to a quill pen, allowing 'inks' of nanoparticles to be drawn onto a surface, creating circuits. As of early 2005, the report said, IBM had demonstrated independently controllable arrays of over 4,000 of the probe quills, and arrays of 1 million or more that were not independently addressable had been constructed elsewhere. Before such technology can change the production line, it has to be larger scale, better controlled and cheaper. Of course, the electronics industry is already highly automated so the switch from one technology to another may not have a major direct impact on employment. But indirectly the shift from an older technology to a newer one, particularly if it ends up heralding a paradigm shift from silicon to molecular or quantum computing, could well result in a shake-out of companies. The disruptive impact of emerging technology is one of the factors behind a forecast that up to 40 per cent of the current 550 semiconductor manufacturers will go out of business in the next ten years.[14]

Sensor technology may well affect employment but the obvious areas of application suggest a continuation of existing trends rather than abrupt change. Take agriculture, for example: the linking of forthcoming sensor technology to control of the dispersal of agrochemicals will be a refinement rather than a revolution in crop control techniques. Crops will be self-monitoring and self-dosing, but that will happen on farms where the tractor and the chemical spray long ago did away with manual labourers. Similarly, the shift away from the mass conscript army began decades ago.

Certainly in Europe the focus is on smaller specialist units. The US has been working to develop robotic soldiers for thirty years with limited success and many more years of work is likely to be needed. But the lines of research discussed earlier certainly suggest that pervasive use of sensors, whether integrated into uniform and equipment or deployed as autonomous swarms, could reduce the use of foot soldiers.

Corporate concentration

From car making to banking, mergers and acquisitions are bringing ever greater consolidation of economic power into fewer and fewer corporate hands. Some thirty of the world's biggest economic entities are companies not countries. Mention has already been made of the concentration of the so-called 'life sciences' into half a dozen multinationals. The chemicals and pharmaceuticals industries have been through a major phase of restructuring, for example bringing about the creation of the vast GlaxoSmithKline empire as Glaxo Wellcome and SmithKline Beecham (themselves the results of series of takeovers) joined forces, and the creation of Aventis through the merger of Hoechst and Rhone-Poulenc in 1999, only to be acquired by Sanofi. The 1990s saw the beginning of a wave of mergers in the energy sector with BP marrying with Amoco, Exxon acquiring Mobil, Chevron merging with Texaco, and Phillips with Conoco. By 2001, thirty-two grocery retailers accounted for 34 per cent of global food retail sales, with the top ten accounting for more than half of that percentage.

In 1998 merger transactions reported to anti-trust agencies in the US were worth some $2,000 billion, against a 1989 previous peak of $600 billion. The volume and value of transactions then fell off for several years against a background of economic downturn.

Merger and acquisition activity is now resurgent. In February 2005 the financial press was full of reports from US banks, corporate finance groups and other market watchers of a renewed appetite for takeovers as consumer product manufacturer Procter & Gamble made a $57 billion move on Gillette, opening debate about the future of another household name, Anglo-Dutch giant Unilever. The European media industry was expected to see more consolidation in 2005 while, over a longer time period, the pressure has been on and will continue to be on semiconductor manufacturers. The UN reported a recovery of world foreign direct investment levels after three years of decline and said mergers and acquisitions would fuel further expansion in the medium term.

This is important for the development of nanotechnology because many of the sectors mentioned above – and particularly pharmaceuticals, electronics, energy and chemical – are those where the emerging technology will take root as and when it develops beyond early iterations as a new ingredient for sun creams, golf balls or paints.

The concentration of market share and capital brings with it a concentration of research and development funding and of capacity to appropriate external research breakthroughs by buying up start-up companies, sponsoring university research work and exercising political leverage over government regulatory and funding decisions.

Multinationals the corporations may be but they are, of course, overwhelmingly creatures of the OECD countries. Be it (non-state) oil companies, food manufacturers, semiconductor makers, pharmaceuticals groups or agrochemical companies, their home base, their primary investors, and their main markets are in the developed world, albeit with growing markets among the middle classes of the industrialising cities of the developing world. The reason for this scarcely needs spelling out: the companies orient themselves and their products towards the most profitable markets. That militates towards the realisation of the Parisian street tableau and not the imaginary African village.

Of course, if nanotechnology products can be expected to be geared towards enhancing the computerisation of Western consumerism before provision of cheap basic communication equipment to schools in the developing world and prioritise the treatment of obesity-related illnesses in North America over malaria in Africa, that is not to say that the developing world will not be used to manufacture nanotechnology products or to offload them. Just as the costs of environmental requirements, health and safety, and labour (as well as much reduced transport costs) have encouraged even medium-size European and North American manufacturers to relocate factories to Asia, so we can be reasonably sure that if manufacturing with nanoparticles proves hazardous it will be carried out in the developing world. The electronics industry is well embedded in the developing world – and not just in the Tiger economies of Southeast Asia. The journal of the Asia Monitor Research Center noted in 2003: 'Semiconductor manufacturing is one of the most hazardous and polluting industries. Yet not many people know about it as the smokeless manufacturing units are generally perceived to be "very clean and safe".' It continued:

> Semiconductor and other electronic hi-tech industries are mushrooming in Asia and more companies from the West are shifting operations to Asia. There is very little known about what happens to workers' health due to the secretive and anti-union attitude of the industry. However, some effects on workers' and community health are emerging. For example, there have been cases of mysterious deaths and disease in the Electronic Industrial Zone, Lamphun, Thailand, and hazardous chemicals from RCA plant in Taiwan have caused cancers and other illnesses among workers and neighbouring communities, who are struggling against these corporations.[15]

Patent power

The patent system will further entrench the control over nano-technology of those companies of the OECD that dominate research and development or have the wherewithal to acquire user licences.

In the chapter on investment in nanotechnology it was noted that the accessing of patented information is frequently character-ised by horse trading between players, a process that disadvantages those with little to bargain with. It was also noted that there has been a concentration of plant patenting so that just a handful of companies are more and more dominating so-called intellectual property 'rights'. Given the structure of the emerging nanotech-nology sector (or industry segments) with the dominance of the rich countries of North America, Europe and developed Asia, the situation is likely to be replicated.

The volume of patent applications relating to nanotechnology has boomed. The first patent for the atomic force microscope, a basic tool in nanoscience, was issued in 1988. Six years later some 100 patents related to the tool were issued per year. By 2003 it was nearer 500.[16] The same trend was apparent for quantum dots and dendrimers. A global database search in late 2004 revealed almost 3,000 patents employing the term 'nanoparticle' and over 2,200 for the term 'nanotube'.

There was a lack of coordination in the approach of govern-ment agencies as biotechnology emerged as a major industry, and there has been a lack of preparedness to deal with nanotechnology too. As late as 2004, the US Patent and Trademark Office not only had no plans to set up a dedicated nanotechnology team but there was no work being done to prepare a classification system for nanotechnology despite the concatenation of related patent applications. This meant the agency could neither reliably track the number of applications nor ensure uniform handling of comparable applications.[17]

The rationale for patenting is that it ensures that the investment of time and money by the inventor and investor is rewarded. If an invention were freely usable by anyone there would be no incentive for individuals or corporations to sink funds and expertise into research and development. The pharmaceuticals industry is one which particularly argues this line, saying that new drugs cost vast sums to develop and require trials lasting many years. For generic drug manufacturers to be able to produce immediately the result of such large investment would remove all incentive to research. The share price of pharmaceuticals companies is frequently linked to the expiry date of patents on key drugs.

The system is also intended to protect the start-up company and the lone inventor. For small companies a strategy for licensing out of products or techniques they have patented along the way can determine whether they survive. Venture capital group 3i cites the view of Liquids Research that 'if you haven't the resources to prepare, obtain or protect a patent, the whole notion can be an unacceptable drain' and the better strategy is to exchange patent rights for guaranteed contract work.[18]

The opposite view has long been taken by Carbon Nanotechnolgies (CNI), where in 2002 the chief executive said, 'We have three PhDs who do nothing but the research to support our patents', as well as an in-house lawyer and two outside law firms.[19] Three years later a public announcement by CNI demonstrated that the company was not simply guarding its hard-earned discoveries but seeking to dominate the carbon nanotube market. It had garnered thirty patents that 'provide an over-arching position in all currently recognised, commercially viable methods of nanotube production, including the electric arc, laser vaporisation, supported catalyst, gas phase and seeded growth processes'.

It is not only companies that seek patent protection. Increasingly commercialised university departments do the same and, according to the ETC Group, the US armed forces have proved particularly aggressive in this regard. The global enforcement of the patent system is entrusted to the World Trade Organisation, which has overseen globalisation of trade and services since it was created out of the old General Agreement on Tariffs and Trade in 1995. In recent years the issue of patents has been mired in controversy over two issues: developing-country access to medicines, particularly HIV/Aids treatments; and the patenting of genetic material.

With millions suffering from HIV/Aids in the developing world and unable to afford treatments patented and produced by the West's pharmaceutical giants, the interpretation and implementation of Article 31 of the Trade-Related Aspects of Intellectual Property Rights (TRIPS) Agreement came into focus. Article 31 is the heavily caveated section of the agreement that permits a country to waive permission from and payment to patent holders 'in the case of a national emergency or other circumstances of extreme urgency or in cases of public non-commercial use'. It seemed unarguable that for many countries HIV/Aids constitutes a national emergency but for lots of those countries the waiver was useless as they had no affordable access to the drugs required. After a massive international campaign, developing countries achieved a victory on two fronts. First, the multinational drugs companies agreed to supply proprietary treatments more cheaply (in order to guard market share). Second, it was agreed at the WTO in August 2003 that those developing countries with established and competent generic drugs industries would be permitted to export to those without indigenous capacity, an option previously blocked by a subsection of the Article.

The other major controversy around global patents concerns the ethical, scientific and social issues around the patenting of living organisms.[20] Leaving aside the issue of Western companies using patent law to seize control of seed varieties developed over generations by farmers in developing countries, campaigners argue that: living organisms should not be treated in the same way as technical developments but constitute a heritage and resource for everyone; that gene sequences are not conventional chemicals but rather living programmes with multifarious functions that should not be controlled like a single-purpose product; that patents on genetic material hinder access to information needed for medical and agricultural advancement.

If nanotechnology yields major advances in, say, the fields of medicine or environmental remediation that its proponents foresee, one can envisage similar controversies arising. Notwithstanding the conditions that must be satisfied in order to win a patent – that the 'invention' must not have been anticipated in previous work; that it is not inherent in a prior invention; that it is not 'obvious' – nanotechnology appears to offer plenty of scope for companies with large legal teams to secure patents over the building blocks of the emerging processes and materials. In doing so they will be seeking licence fees or control over the downstream application of those processes and materials. Where the control is exercised over sports equipment or cosmetics it may raise few social equity concerns but if it stunts the development of medicines for the world's poor it is unacceptable and will surely bring further debate over the provisions of the TRIPS Agreement.

At the philosophical or ethical level, the extension of capital's control right down to the basic building blocks of living organisms may be inherent in a system that battles to assert its control over labour, environment and culture, but for some it breaches a taboo. Widespread assertion of patents over nanoparticles widens the breach because it not only threatens to police access to the results of research into organic nanoscience such as the work using

DNA for computing or for directing molecules but also reaches into the realm of the inorganic such as the nanoscale properties of gold or titanium dioxide.

8

Convergence of technologies: raising the stakes

The development of a product using new techniques or materials by no means guarantees adoption of either the product or the techniques or materials. How many books and films have lampooned 'mad' inventors churning out devices nobody wants? By the same token, how many developers of apparently redundant or inappropriate inventions riposted that their time will come, that society is lagging the opportunities offered by science.

The computer most familiar to us sits on a desk at work or home and is sold by the tens of millions, yet, famously, a generation ago the view was that the market for computers could be counted on the fingers of two hands. The Internet was developed by the US military as an information management and dissemination tool, again with no wide applications foreseen. Its growth has been exponential and its social, political and economic impact profound.

The point here is that if a product, technique or material is to succeed it needs to chime with a perceived demand or it may fall by the wayside or spend years in obscurity or niche applications. It may be, for example, that the massive parallelism potentially offered by quantum computing is not taken up outside of important but niche encryption applications, in part because of an inability to transpose its power and its operational paradigm to extant applications. Of course, there may be other reasons why such a technology was not taken up or why its take-up was delayed, not least electronics manufacturer resistance to a new technology that threatened their vast current investment.

In an emerging area of technology such as nanotechnology there will probably be many culs-de-sac. Some of the research and development money will prove to have been spent on products that do not work or are less efficient and more expensive than competing products. Others will be superseded. There is already a swathe of different approaches to commercialising computer memory based on nanotechnologies, with different companies backing one or more. One industry study lists seven different approaches and reports that a survey showed those deemed most likely to succeed were further from commercialisation while MRAM and FRAM, already in small-scale production, were deemed least likely.[1]

While there is competitive interaction between products and techniques, there is of course also complementarity. The desktop computer combines electronics with software engineering, plastics and telecommunications. Various qualities of materials at the nano-scale will complement each other in products ranging from cars to medicines, foods to weaponry, in the coming years.

The complementarity extends beyond the bounds of nano-technology itself and into what is known as convergence of technologies. That the agrochemical giants are already interweaving nanotechnology with genetic engineering has already been mentioned. The US Future Soldier progamme melds nanotechnology and robotics. DNA computing projects clearly draw on biotech-nology, and the very instrumentation needed for visualising and manipulating material at the nanoscale depends on information technology. Nanotechnology will interact – is interacting – with other broad emerging technologies and this will increase and exacerbate the impact, desirable or undesirable, that it will have on society.

Artificial intelligence (AI) projects would clearly benefit from the enhanced and miniaturised computing capacity offered by nanotechnology both within the silicon-based paradigm and beyond. For some, the development of AI prompts nightmare scenarios as apocalyptic as the 'grey goo' vision. In a famous article for *Wired* magazine, Bill Joy, co-founder of Sun Microsystems and very well known within his industry and beyond, outlined fears engendered by AI, nanotechnology and genetic engineering. Of his life's work in computing, he wrote:

> But now, with the prospect of human-level computing power in about 30 years, a new idea suggests itself: that I may be working to create tools which will enable the construction of the technology that may replace our species.... Given the incredible power of these new technologies, shouldn't we be asking how we can best coexist with them? And if our own extinction is a likely, or even possible, outcome of our technological development, shouldn't we proceed with great caution?[2]

The speed and direction taken by AI developers is probably not leading in the direction of a race of hominoid robots any more than the transformation of the planet into 'grey goo' is a present danger, but that does not negate the need for caution.

The potential applications of nanotechnology and AI hybrids are too numerous to mention but some are clear causes for concern. The *New York Times* reported:

> The Pentagon predicts that robots will be a major fighting force in the American military in less than a decade, hunting and kill- ing enemies in combat. Robots are a crucial part of the Army's

effort to rebuild itself as a 21st-century fighting force, and a $127 billion project called Future Combat Systems is the biggest military contract in American history.

The military plans to invest tens of billions of dollars in automated armed forces. The costs of that transformation will help drive the Defense Department's budget up almost 20 percent, from a requested $419.3 billion for next year to $502.3 billion in 2010, excluding the costs of war. The annual costs of buying new weapons is scheduled to rise 52 percent, from $78 billion to $118.6 billion.[3]

The report goes on to make the point that while these robot soldiers may start off 'looking and acting like lethal toy trucks', as they evolve they may take many different forms and that 'with the development of nanotechnology … they may become swarms of "smart dust".'

The interface between nanosensors and AI will be crucial to the ability to monitor and analyse daily life as revealed by increasingly pervasive tagging of consumer products from food packaging to clothing to vehicles and the plastic in our wallets. Nanosensors will provide the data that will be interpreted and acted upon by artificial intelligence programmes, enhanced by nanoscience-based computing, to decide whether we 'require' further goods, services, medical attention or attention from the security agencies. The UK supermarket chain Tesco has already attracted calls for a consumer boycott through its experimental use of radio frequency identification tags on selected goods at trial stores. Other multinational companies, including the recently merged Gillette and Proctor & Gamble, are experimenting with RFID, which even now employs computer chips no larger than a grain of sand.[4]

In 2004, an independent working group commissioned by the European Commission's Directorate on Knowledge-based Economy and Society, examined the implications of convergence of a range of emerging technologies, among them nanotechnology, biotechnology, information technology, and cognitive and neuroscience. It began by noting that, 'If these various technologies created controversy and anxiety each on their own, their convergence poses a major challenge not only to the research community, but from the very beginning also to policy makers and European societies.'[5]

The document is fascinating because it locates technological development as a determinant of how those with access to it view themselves and their environment. It identifies a set of characteristics associated with the current convergence and their implications.[6]

The convergent technologies will be embedded, which is to say spatially distributed, pervasive and inconspicuous rather than discrete items, so 'our experience of these will be as part of our existence along the lines of climate-controlled buildings or the electric grid'.[7] They will become part of the infrastructure of the lives of those living in rich countries, part of an artificial environment. But this embeddedness 'challenges traditional boundaries between nature and culture.… It makes first nature inaccessible except through a humanly conditioned world.… It dramatically alters our sense of responsibility for the world we live and act in.' The paper points to the 'effects on the sense of reality' that computer gaming and Internet surfing has already had on frequent users' individual and group understanding as a precursor of the social effects of technology convergence.

It is worth recalling the comments made earlier about the danger that promises of environmental remediation through nanotechnology might foster a view of the environment as a commodity that could be fixed when it breaks. This is reflected in another of the characteristics identified in the paper – unlimited reach, the possibility of physically engineering everything, including behaviour. Increasingly sophisticated intervention in the working of the body and brain will mean that both 'will be an explicit or implicit design target of converging technologies'.[8] What implications will this have for morality and notions of self? If the mind can be engineered, who is responsible, morally or legally, for the actions of the engineered individual? And what of the implications of the prosthetics and performance-enhancing fixes that can be envisaged – the muscles grown from biocompatible nanomaterials, operated through advanced robotics informed by nanosensors and controlled by AI? Clearly, access to these would be a boon of sorts to the physically disabled but what expectations of physical 'perfection' will they engender and how great will become the divide between those with and those without the high-technology gadgets? Will society come to accept or expect enhancements to all bodies, and what implications does this have for our sense of ourselves as imperfect, mortal but nonetheless individual creatures? More trivially, where does it leave sports? Is an athlete who has replaced a damaged cartilage with a better, stronger, artificial version still allowed to compete?

9

Taming the genie

Nanotechnology is a fast-moving area of science on the cusp of major commercialisation, which will bring it into more and more aspects of the daily lives of people living in rich countries as well as the burgeoning middle classes in the high-tech zones of the developing world.

Whatever the past debates, the term is used more and more to cover a range of products, research paths and processes that have in common the deliberate manipulation or employment of materials in order to harness particular qualities exhibited at the nanoscale, that is to say smaller than one-billionth of a metre, a size where quantum physics kicks in. Those properties might be electrical conductivity, reactivity to light, enhanced catalytic qualities, strength combined with light weight, or ability to attract or repel other materials. The very breadth of potential applications, from computing to medicine, environmental remediation, energy supply and warfare, suggests that nanotechnology will seep into our lives from a number of different sources. Sometimes we will be aware of it because it will be heralded. Other times we will have no such knowledge. Indeed, already nanoscale materials are being used in consumer items from clothing to cosmetics, sports equipment to computer memory, yet how many consumers are aware of this unless the manufacturer uses the fact as a marketing tool?

Nuclear power was to solve the world's energy needs and genetically modified crops (like the Green Revolution a generation earlier) were to feed the world. Nanotechnology reaches across sectors and disciplines, informing those working on fuel cells, water filtration, manufacturing or information technology, and so the optimist's dream is that nanotechnology might help to solve not just one of the crises facing global society but all of them. Recall the US Congress member quoted in the early pages of this book who compared the advent of nanotechnology to the transition from the Stone Age to the Bronze Age. For the enthusiast, it offers cures for the diseases that haunt us and the environmental disasters we visit upon ourselves, while providing us with yet more goods and services and comforts.

It is important not to lose sight of those hopes and ambitions. The transformative potential of nanotechnology for the lives not just of those in the rich world and its overseas enclaves but for the poor and dispossessed does look to be impressive. Solar power for those dependent on biomass, potable water for all, fast diagnosis of illnesses even many miles from a laboratory, smog-free streets and reclaimed land – all would-be life-savers for millions across the world.

Yet is this where current nanotechnology research and development is leading? Will the Parisian street tableau and the Sahelian village tableau coexist? As things stand – and that is an important qualifying phrase – the answers look disheartening.

Development of nanotechnology is centred, as one would expect, in the developed world's universities, corporations and institutions. It is in the US and the EU and Japan that government funds have been found to support nanotechnology research. It is the corporations of the rich world that have the expertise and the money to devote to in-house or arm's-length research projects and to gain control over the advances made by others, whether through sponsoring them, buying them out or licensing them.

It reflects well on the partner in a venture capital company quoted in an interview in an industry newsletter who said his personal priority for nanotechnology applications would be 'Any applications that exponentially improve the lives of humans, especially those in less developed parts of the world.'[1] But the question put to him was, what area would he fund *if* he could follow his passion rather than return on investment? And there is the rub.

The Meridian Institute, a non-profit-making body in the US with the mission of 'connecting people to solve problems', has convened a global dialogue on nanotechnology and the poor. In a preparatory paper[2] the institute noted:

1. Most industrial-country governments and a number of governments in the developing world are investing in nanotechnology but 'even in countries where a large proportion of citizens are poor, little of this investment is going to benefits for the poor'.
2. Aid agencies are not generally involved in funding or guidance of nanotechnology.
3. Most government investments are aimed at improving the competitiveness of locally based corporations rather than focusing on benefits for the poor.
4. Just as the first fruit of genetic engineering of plants was not drought-resistant varieties for impoverished peasant farmers but rather crops with resistance that tied them to proprietary agrochemicals, so the first products of nanotechnology are tennis balls and sunblock not cheaper energy and purer water.

5. The rush to patent nanotechnology threatens to slow innovation, drive up costs and restrict access to knowledge that could
alleviate suffering.

The adage that he who pays the piper calls the tune applies to
emerging technologies. Inasmuch as nanotechnology research and
development is controlled by companies and investors motivated
by profits, and governments motivated by maintaining and extend-
ing their economic, political and military power, so profits and
power will dictate the applications of the R&D. It is a reasonable
assumption that antidepressants and anti-obesity treatments for the
OECD market will take precedence over combating diseases of
the developing world and that lightweight weaponry will attract
more interest than improved agricultural implements.

That is not to deny that there are initiatives to involve developing countries, whether through their governments or civil society,
in emerging technologies. Then there are developing countries like
India that are carrying out valuable research in their own institutions. The EU provides funds for technology transfer, for example.
The UN Industrial Development Organisation held a conference
in early 2005 to examine how developing countries could build
a relevant capability in nanotechnology. It is likely that the current boardroom vogue for 'corporate responsibility' will see some
major companies ensuring they win kudos for sponsoring some
new technology applications in developing countries.

Nonetheless, as with any new technology, the unequal challenge
posed by the emergence of nanotechnology is to appropriate it for
the general good rather than the greater wealth of shareholders
in giant corporations, the further gratification of advertising-led
consumer demands in wealthy countries, and enhanced power of
overmighty governments. When considering this challenge it must
be borne in mind that access to new technology is not a panacea

for social ills, even if it may be a palliative. The Meridian Institute paper states concisely one of the lessons of technology transfer over the past fifty years:

> Technology, to work, must be part of a demand-driven solution, not 'the solution'. To work well, solutions must fit into the habits, norms, aspirations, laws, knowledge base, resource base, and regulatory systems of the societies into which they are inserted.[3]

Yet even when technology is implanted successfully it remains something introduced from outside, a beneficial transfer of the fruits of technology but not of the technology itself, for that remains locked in the knowledge base, laboratories and patent filings of the originating country or company.

One further consideration: an improvement of the lives of the world's impoverished may in some cases be a necessary condition for their empowerment, but it does not constitute it. Water purification technology does not stop the nearby Coca-Cola plant draining and polluting the aquifer. Communities may benefit greatly from hand-held diagnostic devices, but the devices do not prevent the illnesses caused by polluting factories or disastrous drainage projects. Giving a farmer a better range of tools does not give him land.

So, the first of the fundamental questions this book is intended to pose to the reader is: how can the advances promised by nanotechnology be prevented from being the preserve of the wealthy countries and the wealthier strata of the developing countries, and how can those advances be steered in directions that are appropriate to the needs and contributory to the empowering of the poor? If the first question addresses the equitable distribution of the potential benefits of nanotechnology, the second addresses the potential dangers it poses. How should nanotechnology be controlled?

Neither of the questions finds an answer here but the following pages corral some of the issues that require consideration. And, platitudinous though it has become to say it, consideration and debate is urgently required. The mantric call for public discussion and involvement began with those non-governmental organisations that have long been concerned with nanotechnology, from the Foresight Institute to the ETC Group and the Center for Responsible Nanotechnology. More recently it has been a vital ingredient in any list of recommendations in government and government-sponsored reports. More recently still, the need to involve developing-country governments and NGOs has also been recognised. Achieving that is more difficult than saying it. There are a handful of initiatives in the developing world where attempts are being made to tailor nanotechnology to local needs, but much more is needed. It is incumbent upon the independent, transnational networks of the labour, consumer and environmental movements to provide information and encourage debate.

There are different levels at which the potential dangers of nanotechnology require consideration. Some have proposed relinquishment or at least a moratorium on development. Lower tiers of control range from the outlawing and international policing of some applications down to the reformulation of health and safety at work legislation or conventions on the labelling of products.

The arguments for relinquishment of nanotechnology – for locking it in a Pandora's box – derive in large part from the fear of 'grey goo', an Armageddon of replicators unleashed by design or accident. In his essay 'Why the Future Doesn't Need Us',[4] Bill Joy uses the Pandora's box analogy and argues for a re-evaluation of our fundamental belief that knowledge is good, saying: 'if open access to and unlimited development of knowledge henceforth puts us all in clear danger of extinction, then common sense demands that we re-examine even these basic, long-held beliefs.' He calls for relinquishment of genetic engineering, nanotechnology and advanced robotics, saying that action to ensure non-proliferation of nuclear weaponry and towards nuclear arms reduction by the countries holding them gives cause to believe relinquishment is possible. (Joy was writing before India and Pakistan demonstrated that they had nuclear weapons and does not mention that Israel has long had an arsenal in flagrant contravention of international law.)

The ETC Group calls for a halt to nanotechnology research and development. It advances two main grounds for this: that there has not been adequate investigation or regulation of the dangers posed by nanoscale particles; and that there has not been public debate over the potential social consequences of the new technology. This is distinct from Joy's position and constitutes an application of the 'precautionary principle'. ETC Group calls for a code of best practice to be adopted by governments, full involvement of society before nanotechnology is unleashed, and the establishment of an international body to monitor new technologies.[5]

As Drexler and others have ceased preaching the 'grey goo' peril, so the argument for relinquishment has been weakened although some argue that the dangers of 'green goo' – runaway replication of nano-engineered biological matter – are just as frightening and more feasible.

One of the arguments advanced against relinquishment is that when something is outlawed all those engaged in it immediately become outlaws. A body of hitherto law-abiding people become criminals overnight. Those who persist in the activity – in this case research and development – do so in secret and therefore cannot be regulated. Better to regulate than ban, moderate the risk rather than eliminate it in most places most of the time but have it continue uncontrolled somewhere sometimes. Advocates of this position would describe themselves as pragmatists. The same argument could be advanced for permitting promiscuous development of weapons of mass destruction. Indeed, one paper advocating control of nanotechnology rather than relinquishment argued:

> A prohibitionist approach that entirely blocks nanotechnology research will prevent any harm at severe cost. But a protectionist approach that prevents 99.999 per cent of research, while allowing, say, a few underground projects sponsored by rogue states to slip through its net, will do just as much harm but no good. Indeed, it may actually make things worse since those rogue states will then hold a monopoly on a powerful technology, while the civilised world will lack the wherewithal to deploy countermeasures.[6]

Replace the term 'nanotechnology' with 'nuclear weapons' and this reasoning, complete with its imperialistic world-view, is immediately familiar.

Perhaps more compelling and no less pragmatic rather than principled is the argument that the genie is already out of the bottle and that the governments of the world have been so laggardly in discussing oversight of nanotechnology internally, let alone collectively, that the opportunity to impose a global ban or even moratorium on nanotechnology has been and gone. Absent multilateral action, no government of a country with a serious nanotechnology research base is going to forgo the potential economic and other gains; however much they may nod to the precautionary principle in worthy addresses on the future of the planet. As we have seen, the list of companies and countries involved in nanotechnology is long and ever growing. It takes years to negotiate international conventions and, as the Kyoto process on climate change demonstrated, more years to win ratification let alone application. The forecast take-off of nanotechnology as a major generator of revenue is on a shorter timescale. Once profits are being made, governments are not going to consider relinquishment or even a broad moratorium except in the face of compelling evidence of extraordinary harm.

The Center for Responsible Nanotechnology, which concentrates on 'advanced nanotechnology' – molecular manufacturing – and believes it to be nearer to realisation than do many others, puts forward a positive reason to reject relinquishment. It says the strongest argument against is that it would mean forgoing or at least delaying 'the potential to reduce stress on the environment, to alleviate most shortages, to raise living standards worldwide, to eradicate nearly all poverty, starvation and homelessness'.[7] This argument is, of course, only as compelling as one's conviction that nanotechnology can or will be harnessed to such ends.

Where civil society may well be able to intervene and force action from governments individually and collectively is in the control and regulation of nanotechnology. Such control can range from the narrow focus of workplace health and safety through to demands for a global ban on particular applications. Beginning with the narrower focus, it is incumbent on the labour movement and the consumer movement to work with environmental campaigners to push governments towards a 'cradle to grave' approach to goods and processes employing nanotechnology. The materials and processes employed in the production process must be thoroughly audited. The loopholes must be closed that allow a material at the nanoscale to evade fresh testing because it has been tested at a larger scale, even though the very rationale for its use at nanoscale is that its properties are different.

The Nanoforum report on the benefits and risks of nanotechnology described regulation in the EU countries as being in its infancy. It may be China that first applies national standards for nanomaterials. The *People's Daily* reported that such standards would be imposed on seven materials from April 2005 because 'some businesses play tricks and consumers get confused'.[8] However, the thrust appeared to be ensuring smoother development of business rather than worker or consumer safety.

It was late 2004 before the first international gathering of occupational health experts was convened in Britain, under the auspices of the Health and Safety Executive and its US counterpart, the National Institute for Occupational Safety and Health. The attendees agreed that not enough was known and that much more research was needed. Meanwhile, they recommended use of traditional forms of risk assessment. NIOSH is working on a strategic plan to address the health and safety at work aspects of nanotechnology, but it is doing so within the framework of the National Nanotechnology Initiative, the driving aim of which is to ensure the US is a global leader in the new technology. In Britain, the government eventually responded in part to the Royal Society study it had commissioned. But all it promised was a review of current safety regulations and a cross-government body to evaluate safety-related research. The reaction from the Royal Society was one of disappointment, noting the government 'does not dedicate any new money for the research which will be essential to support the development of robust regulations'.[9]

The goods produced using nanomaterials must be tested more thoroughly than they are now. The lack of regulation is recognised by those developing products. The chief executive of one UK nanotechnology company was quoted as saying: 'There are gaps in the regulations that need to be filled. We are doing toxicology tests in the absence of a regulatory framework.'[10] With so little research on the migration of nanoscale particles into and through the body, it cannot be acceptable that current nanotechnology applications such as skin products and cosmetics are not subject to the same scrutiny as medicines. To date, the most effective voice in raising such concerns has been from the insurance industry rather than the consumer movement, despite the latter's enormous success (in Europe) over genetically modified food.

Appropriate regulation may speed realisation of benefits of nanotechnology as well as circumventing dangers. The European Science Foundation looked at the prospects for nanotechnology in medicine. It called for a case-by-case approach to clinical and regulatory evaluation and said, 'Further development of appropriate regulatory requirements, approval processes and organisation is essential to facilitate the safe and swift introduction of future nanomedicines.'[11]

The principle of labelling goods and so allowing consumers to select a product according to its ingredients has now been established in Europe with the implementation of a broad if imperfect regime for GM foods. The principle should surely be applied to goods containing nanomaterials. There may well be resistance from the US government and from manufacturers of sensitive goods such as food, food packaging, and cosmetics, although makers of outdoor clothing or sport equipment or computers might well want to trumpet the cutting-edge technology behind their water-resistant, higher bouncing, bigger-memory products.

Also demanding consideration is what happens to goods containing nanoscale materials once they are disposed of. There is a working assumption that once bound into composites – as in car panels, for example – nanomaterials are unlikely to pose any hazard. This assumption needs to be tested before the composites begin to fill dumps and incinerators. Certainly any potential for the release into the environment of unbound nanoparticles, let alone those with a biological component, must not be permitted until much more is known of their long-term impact on soil, water, air and animal life. Already, assumptions that fullerenes could not be transported in water have proven false. The promise of environmental remediation using nanoparticles is alluring but environmentalists will surely want to resist it until the full course of the particles has been thoroughly documented. Encouragingly, academic research is being conducted to evaluate the environmental impact of nanomaterial waste and to determine if it can be treated before it enters the environment to negate this impact.

It is critical that social movements that engage in the regulation of nanotechnology do so internationally. Experience teaches all too well the willingness of companies and governments to export dangerous manufacturing processes, substandard goods, and toxic wastes to the developing world or to lax regulatory regimes from the more rigorous.

The logic of the argument that relinquishment is impractical once a technological cat is out of the laboratory bag would seem to apply as much to partial relinquishment – the banning of particular areas of research or types of application – as it does to a total ban. Indeed, one might argue that it is even more impractical. If, say, non-military research and development is permitted, surely it is more difficult to prevent leakage of expertise into proscribed military applications whether illicitly or with the covert or indeed overt approval of governments.

Yet we do have international conventions and laws proscribing nuclear proliferation and chemical and biological weapons. These are more or less imperfect and, as we know to our cost, are applied selectively – Israel is allowed to maintain a nuclear arsenal, Iraq was invaded in large part on the pretext it had weapons of mass destruction when it did not. Nonetheless, the international community accepts the principle of selective bans on technology and has mechanisms through which to police the principle. Similarly, governments have moved at varying paces and in varying directions on ethical problems posed by genetics, developing positions on stem-cell research and human embryology.

That being the case, there is room for discussion and action over selective bans on nanotechnology. Military applications seem an obvious candidate for debate. We do not have to look as far as 'smart dust' nanobots capable of offensive operations – and some believe this to be as little as a decade away – to find a case for an immediate ban. Indian scientists have pointed out the imminent viability of weapons exploiting the size of nanoparticles to attack the lungs of target populations or forces, to encourage development of tumours through the generation of free radicals, or to breed and release engineered viruses. As an article in *India Daily* remarked: 'Armies of enormous strengths can be wiped out slowly without even fighting a single battle. The soldiers may never know that they have been nano-poisoned.'[12]

The reluctance of nuclear powers to give up their arsenals has severely cramped attempts to create a legal ban on weapons of mass destruction. Their use is controlled in general by various international laws and agreements, including the Geneva Conventions; yet, as the International Committee of the Red Cross has noted, 'these principles and rules have to be supplemented by more precise instruments in order to clarify and take into account all their implications for the use of a specific weapon.'[13] However, chemical and biological weapons are dealt with specifically by three international agreements, including the 1993 Chemical Weapons Convention that provides for policing the pact. Disarmament campaigners need to consider whether the terms of existing laws are broad enough to embrace various types of nanoscale weaponry. If so, this needs to be made explicit. If not, urgent action is required.

Civil libertarians have cause for alarm at the potential for increased state and corporate surveillance and control implied by the melding of nanotechnology and artificial intelligence. Population profiling will become infinitely more sophisticated and pervasive with the proliferation of ever smaller and more complex tagging and data processing. Without limits being put on the use of tagging and sensors and, perhaps even more crucially, on the sharing of data collected, there is the clear potential for unprecedented intrusion into our lives whether it be to check if a mental patient in the community is taking medication, if a social security recipient is living beyond their legal means, to track foreign citizens entering a country, or seek out marketing opportunities. Vigilance over state use of telephone tapping and spyware infiltration of personal computers will be as nothing compared with the attention needed to maintain civil liberties in societies where more and more aspects of life are mediated by new technologies.

A rather more crude concern for civil libertarians is the indication that the military and security apparatus intends to use nanotechnology for the development of 'non-lethal' weapons, those most likely to be deployed against civilian populations at home or abroad. In 2004, a US campaigning group was instructed by the Marine Corps to remove from its website military documents detailing development of 'chemical immobilizers' and 'anti-personnel calmative agents' that may have exploited nanoparticles.

If these and perhaps other types of applications raise the case for partial bans, there are others where the case may be made for a moratorium, pending full discussion of the social and ethical implications.

The potential contribution of nanotechnology to the provision of tougher, lighter, more responsive prosthetics from replacement hips to corneas is exciting. So is the opportunity for the development of better medicines, delivered to the right part of the body or brain in quantities suited to the individual patient. But the advances held out by nanomedicine also raise issues of rights and identity. In mental health, replace the 'chemical cosh' with more tailored, more subtle forms of intervention in the individual human brain and it becomes more difficult to determine when an individual's actions and thoughts are his or her own. Combine this with a society where experience of the environment is more and more mediated by technology and one can quickly conjure up a nightmare vision of individuals in a permanently chemically altered state of mind whose perception of the world is ever more mediated by increasingly sophisticated virtual realities within a cocoon of regulated sensory experience. The legal and ethical issues here demand debate beyond the medical profession, pharmaceuticals industry and the studies of moral philosophers such as Dany-Robert Dufour.[14]

The case for cradle-to-grave regulation and application of the precautionary principle has already been put within the narrower focus. But perhaps it needs to be posed more broadly. Rather than just assessing individual products from construction to disposal, it may be that there is an argument for banning the introduction into the environment by any means of any artificial nanoparticle for which the migratory potential is not fully documented and which cannot be shown to be entirely harmless (a slippery term in itself). Consideration of this question would, of course, also include substances that the current state of knowledge suggests could be of great help in cleaning up the mess created by previous technologies. It would explicitly include biological–nanotechnological interface substances that some fear could herald a 'green goo'. It would certainly include any development of self-replicating creations.

Pondering the challenges of control of nanotechnology must not squeeze out the challenge of finding ways in which a regulated nanotechnology can be harnessed for the common good and not just the profits of corporations, the enhanced powers of the state, and the gratification of wealthy consumers.

The market will not provide for the poor and dispossessed of the world because, in their hundreds of millions, they are outside of any profitable market. Different mechanisms are needed. First, it is necessary to identify the demands and needs of potential beneficiaries, to establish appropriate, demand-led solutions to those needs. This requires the active participation of indigenous organisations in developing countries, groups that can articulate the demands while understanding the potential of nanotechnology. The Meridian Institute notes that governments are generally investing in nanotechnology for commercial and 'national' advantage rather than in projects designed to benefit all of society. That is probably true of developing-country governments as well as those of the industrialised world. Indeed, the UN Industrial Development Organisation's North–South dialogue on nanotechnology, reflecting UNIDO's brief, emphasised that nanotechnology was crucial to local enterprises rather than populations.

However, the Institute's report does identify some hopeful developments such as cooperation between India, Brazil and South Africa in HIV/Aids prevention and treatment, including use of nanotechnology. But closer to the notion of articulating the needs of the poor and seeking ways to satisfy them is the South African Nanotechnology Initiative, which seeks to bring together local universities and companies and research organisations to 'establish a critical mass in nanotechnology R&D in South Africa for the benefit of all its citizens'.[15] Among projects it is running are those looking at developing cheaper and better solar cells, nanomembranes for water purification, and fuel cells.

While there is research work going on in some developing countries, the reality is that the overwhelming majority of the work is done in the rich countries of the world and is controlled by corporations and governments. Their control over the technology is underpinned by a patenting system that has been globalised through the World Trade Organisation. The use and elaboration of Article 31 in the case of some medicines was an important victory for developing countries and their allies. The question is whether this can be built on, with a campaign to force the release of technology that can relieve hunger, lack of energy, and disease. In early 2005, a US presidential advisory panel was being assembled to look into imposing export limits on nanotechnology.

A period when the UN system is being undermined both by its very real failings and by the efforts of the US administration is hardly auspicious for the creation of new international agencies. Indeed, the certainty of rejection by Washington has just sabotaged proposals for a UN body on migration. Nonetheless, the case for an international approach to the development and control of nanotechnology is compelling for anyone committed to human safety, environmental integrity and the broad dissemination of the benefits of the emerging technology.

Individual nations or corporations are loath to forgo competitive advantage even when that advantage brings with it dangers to people or environments. Just look at the unwillingness of the UK government to convert pious speeches about global warming and even pledges of emission cuts beyond Kyoto Convention commitments into action. Or consider the refusal to relinquish nuclear weaponry even after the end of the Cold War (except by South Africa). The (short-run) advantages of not raising fuel duty or imposing a higher levy on industrial users of energy may be local but the impact of emissions is global, just as the 'security' provided by nuclear weapons is local but radioactivity knows no frontiers. While national or regional policymakers may be able to find a way around World Trade Organisation rules to keep out GM foods, so they may be able to find ways to keep out nanotechnology products with a high emotive value to consumers. But more broadly, the potential dangers of nanotechnology, if realised, will be global, whether in the shape of fearsome new weapons, pervasive monitoring, environmental degradation, deeper social divisions or reduced demand for the commodities produced by farmers and mineworkers in the developing world.

The assessment of those dangers, the drafting of agreements to eliminate or minimise them, and the policing of the agreements all require a multilateral and inclusive approach. In June 2004, the US convened a meeting of twenty-six governments to discuss the question of how to prepare the world for the emergence of nanotechnology. As the ETC Group remarked, the meeting could hardly be characterised as pre-emptive. Nor could it be exhaustive, with issues such as nanotechnology in developing countries or socio-economic and ethical issues dealt with in subgroups meeting for under two hours. With only a handful of the major players of the developing world in attendance, it was not inclusive either. There is an increasing number of international conferences addressing aspects of nanotechnology and it is heartening that developing-country access is increasingly recognised as an issue for discussion. But it is not enough, not by a long way.

It may be unfair to prejudge a body such as the International Council on Nanotechnology unveiled at Rice University in the US in October 2004 but a body sponsored by DuPont, Proctor & Gamble, Intel, L'Oréal, Mitsubishi, Frontier Carbon Corporation, and Swiss Re does not seem most appropriate to advise on international regulation of nanotechnology. What is needed is not bodies and conferences organised by governments or institutions of the rich countries but rather a forum that is owned by all the countries of the world and where the agenda is not dictated by wealth or control of technology. That suggests a one-nation, one-vote model rather than the contribution-weighted voting that skews the balance of power in some international institutions.

It would be naive, of course, to believe that giving the governments of developing countries equal voting to the rich countries in a global talking shop would equate to any advance in the living conditions of the poor of those developing countries. An international forum is no substitute for the articulation of popular needs within developing countries by civil society within the countries.

The need may well extend beyond a medium for debate and legislation. It may reach into appropriation of technology in order to meet basic needs that nanotechnology can satisfy. If a technology exists that can provide clean water to the hundred of millions who lack it, or bring solar power to the fuel-poor, or provide medical diagnosis in the most remote locations, or mitigate the effects of environmental pollution and climate change, then access to it must not be limited by greed. With or without remuneration, individuals, companies or agencies inventing materials or processes capable of relieving suffering must be forced to share the fruits of progress.

Internationalisation of the management of nanotechnology (and emerging technologies more generally) has been proposed by various organisations. The ETC Group argues that

> Rather than being forced to scramble and react to one technological wave after the other, the international community must create a new body dedicated to track, evaluate and accept or reject new technologies and their products through an International Convention on the Evaluation of New Technologies.[16]

The Center for Responsible Nanotechnology stresses the need for broad participation: 'The only answer is a collective answer, and that will demand an unprecedented collaboration – a network of leaders in business, government, academia, and NGOs. It will require participation from people of many nations, cultures, languages and belief systems.'[17] Elsewhere the CRN maintains that molecular manufacturing will arrive (and soon) and that the safest way to develop it is within a single international project. That approach would minimise the risks while maximising control. An international project could be more secure and reduce the chances of a nanotechnology-driven arms race while preventing corporate monopolies over life-saving technology, it says.[18]

The work done by specialist non-governmental organisations to raise awareness of the global issues raised by nano- and other emerging technologies is invaluable. The proposal that nanotechnology is overseen at the international level makes sense too. The reach of the corporations, governments and markets through which nanotechnology will develop is global and so are the potential benefits and dangers of the new materials and processes. If nanotechnology is to mean cleaner water, provision of energy, rapid diagnosis and available treatments for tropical diseases, and not just more refined temperature controls in the restaurants of European capitals, higher definition televisions and control of obesity in North America, then the poor and their advocates must demand access. By the same token, if nanotechnology is not to become an unprepared-for threat to employment patterns, a new source of occupational illness, a generator of new forms of pollution, a danger to consumers, a threat to civil liberties and the impetus for a new arms race, then civil society must seek to control its development.

Notes

Chapter 1

1. Hearing before the Sub-committee on Basic Research, Committee on Science, US House of Representatives, 22 June 1999.
2. K. Eric Drexler, *Engines of Creation*, Anchor Books, New York, 1990, p. 172.
3. Ibid., p. 176.
4. Testimony of Ray Kurzweil to the Committee on Science, US House of Representatives, 9 April 2003.
5. Philip S. Anton, Richard Silberglitt and James Schneider, *The Global Technology Revolution: Bio/nano/materials Trends and Their Synergies with Information Technology by 2015*, RAND National Defense Research Institute, Santa Monica CA, 2001, p. xvii.
6. *The Big Down: Atomtech – Technologies Converging at the Nanoscale*, ETC Group, Ottawa, 2003, p. 8.
7. *Chemical and Engineering News*, cover story, 1 December 2003.
8. Ed Regis, 'The Incredible Shrinking Man', *Wired*, vol. 12, no. 10, October 2004.
9. *Nanoscience and Nanotechnologies: Opportunities and Uncertainties*, Royal Society and Royal Academy of Engineering, London, July 2004.
10. 'There's Plenty of Room at the Bottom', talk by Richard Feynman at the 1959 annual meeting of the American Physical Society, California Institute of Technology, www.zyvex.com/nanotech/feynman.html.

11. Eric Drexler, 'Nanotechnology: from Feynman to Funding', *Bulletin of Science, Technology and Society*, vol. 24, no. 1, February 2004.
12. Ibid.
13. Lawrence Gasman, *What Will the Future Nanotech Industry Look Like?*, NanoMarkets White Paper series, Sterling VA, March 2004.
14. US Environmental Protection Agency, www.epa.gov/ttn/catc/dir1/fzeolite.pdf, 1998.
15. 'Nanotech Report', Forbes/Wolfe, www.forbesnanotech.com, December 2004.
16. *The Big Down*, pp. 22–4.
17. DG Bank, cited in Axel Ebenau, 'Economic Perspectives of Nanotechnology', speech, BASF, October 2002, available on BASF's website.
18. *The Big Down*, pp. 22–4.
19. Company website.
20. Company website.
21. Ebenau, 'Economic Perspectives of Nanotechnology'.
22. Anton, Silberglitt and Schneider, *The Global Technology Revolution*, p. 23.
23. Stephen Gillett, *Nanotechnology: Clean Energy and Resources for the Future*, Foresight Institute, Palo Alto CA, 2002.
24. *Nanotechnology: Innovation for Tomorrow's World*, European Commission Community Research, Brussels, 2004, p. 39.
25. Company website.
26. Mark Ratner and Daniel Ratner, *Nanotechnology: A Gentle Introduction to the Next Big Idea*, Prentice Hall, Harlow, 2003, pp. 68–9.
27. Bayer, *Research* 15, April 2004, pp. 39–41.
28. Paul Alivisatos, 'Less Is More In Medicine', in *Understanding Nanotechnology*, ed. Scientific American, Warner Books, New York, 2002, p. 62.
29. *Nanoscience and Nanotechnologies*, p. 23.
30. Ibid., p. 17.
31. Ibid.
32. Mark Reed and James Tour, 'Computing with Molecules', in *Understanding Nanotechnology*, p. 113.
33. Ratner and Ratner, *Nanotechnology*, p. 132.
34. Charles Lieber, 'The Incredible Shrinking Circuit', in *Understanding Nanotechnology*, p. 93.
35. Company press release, 9 September 2002.
36. *TMT Trends: Predictions, 2005*, Deloitte Touche Tohmatsu, London, 2005, p. 11.

Chapter 2

1. *21st Century Nanotechnology Research and Development Act*, 108th Congress of the United States of America, 7 January 2003, section 6.
2. indolink.com, 6 November 2004.
3. Carbon Nanotechnologies Inc., press release, 24 January 2002.
4. Nanoinvestornews newsletter, 26 October 2004.
5. *Nanotechnology: Its Impact on Defence and the MOD*, UK Ministry of Defence, London, 2001.
6. Govexec.com, 19 April 2004.
7. *Special Report: Emerging Technologies and Their Impact on Arms Control and Non-proliferation*, Nato Parliamentary Assembly committee report, October 2001.
8. Govexec.com, 31 March 2003.
9. 'Hearing before the Subcommittee on Basic Research of the Committee on Science', US House of Representatives, 106th Congress, 22 June 1999.
10. Paul Williams, *Osama's Revenge: The Next 9/11*, Prometheus Books, 2004, p. 153.
11. Daniel Ratner and Mark Ratner, *Nanotechnology and Homeland Security*, Prentice Hall, Harlow, 2004, p. 68.
12. Ibid., p. 5.
13. MEMS Project Summaries, www.darpa.mil/mto/mems/summaries/projects/dyncorp.
14. Testimony of Ray Kurzweil on the Societal Implications of Nanotechnology, US House of Representatives Committee on Science, 9 April 2003.
15. *Nanotechnology: Its Impact on Defence and the MOD*.
16. 'Field-Deployable Biological Threat Detection System Using Quantum Dots', Evident Technologies, July 2002.
17. *Thoughts on the Economics of Nanosensors*, NanoMarkets White Paper series, Sterling VA, December 2004, p. 7.
18. IST website, http://web.mit.edu/isn/.
19. FFW website, www.natick.army.mil/soldier/WSIT/.
20. John Petersen and Dennis Egan, 'Small Security: Nanotechnology and Future Defense', in Center for Technology and National Security Policy, National Defense University, *Defense Horizons* 8, March 2002.
21. Mark Avrum Gubrud, 'Nanotechnology and International Security',

paper for the Fifth Foresight Conference on Molecular Nanotechnology, 2000, available at www.foresight.org/Conferences/MNT05/Papers/Gubrud/.

Chapter 3

1. Howard Lovy, *Can Nano Create New Markets?*, NanoMarkets White Paper series, Sterling VA, April 2004.
2. Alexander Arnall, *Future Technologies, Today's Choices*, Imperial College London for Greenpeace Environmental Trust, London, July 2003, table 12.
3. 'Benefits, Risks, Ethical, Legal and Social Aspects of Nanotechnology', Nanoforum.org, www.nanoforum.org, June 2004, p. 20.
4. *New Dimensions for Manufacturing: A UK Strategy for Nanotechnology*, Department of Trade and Industry and Office of Science and Technology, London, 2002, p. 22.
5. Testimony of Alan Marty of JP Morgan Partners to US House of Representatives Committee on Science, 19 March 2003; and Arnall, *Future Technologies*, table 11.
6. *New Dimensions for Manufacturing*.
7. *Nanoscience and Nanotechnologies: Opportunities and Uncertainties*, Royal Society and Royal Academy of Engineering, London, 2004, p. 11.
8. *Down on the Farm: The Impact of Nanoscale Technologies on Food and Agriculture*, ETC Group, Ottawa, November 2004, p. 11.
9. *Global Analysis of Nanotechnology in the Automotive Market*, Frost & Sullivan, London, 2004.
10. Press release issued by NanoMarkets, Sterling VA, 7 December 2004.
11. Philip S. Anton, Richard Silberglitt and James Schneider, *The Global Technology Revolution: Bio/nano/materials Trends and Their Synergies with Information Technology by 2015*, RAND National Defense Research Institute, Santa Monica CA, 2001, p. 20.
12. *New Dimensions for Manufacturing*, p. 48.
13. Ibid., p. 22.
14. For example, *Technology Forecast 2002–2004*, vol. 2, PWC Global Technology Research Center, California, p. 72.
15. Anton, Silberglitt and Schneider, *The Global Technology Revolution*, p. 28.
16. *Select Committee on Science and Technology Fifth Report*, United Kingdom Parliament, Stationery Office, London, 2004, part 2 table 1.

17. *New Dimensions for Manufacturing*, p. 22.
18. *Nanoscience and Nanotechnologies*, pp. 22–3.
19. Ibid., p. 27.
20. Cited in 'Economic Perspectives of Nanotechnology: Enormous Markets for Tiny Particles', presentation by Axel Ebenau at 'Journalist and Scientists in Dialogue', Mannheim, Germany, 28–29 October 2002, published by BASF, p. 3.
21. *New Dimensions for Manufacturing*, p. 24 table 1.
22. Semiconductor Industry Association press release, November 2004, www.sia-online.org/pre_release.cfm?ID=338.
23. Extrapolated from *Human Development Report 2004*, United Nations Development Programme, New York, 2004.
24. 'Elevator to the Stars – Scientist Sees Elevator Reaching into Space', Associated Press, 26 June 2004.
25. Testimony of Ray Kurzweil to the Committee on Science, US House of Representatives, 9 April 2003.
26. Ronald Bailey, 'Nanotechnology: Hell or Heaven?', www.reason. com, 27 October 2004.

Chapter 4

1. *Financial Times*, London, 14 July 2004.
2. *Nanotechnology – Size Matters: Building a Successful Nanotechnology Company*, 3i in association with the *Economist* Intelligence Unit and the Institute of Nanotechnology, London, July 2002.
3. *Chemical and Engineering News*, 1 September 2003.
4. *Towards a European Strategy for Nanotechnology*, European Commission, Brussels, COM (2004) 338, section 2, p. 7.
5. *Nano-enabled Drug Delivery Systems Market*, NanoMarkets White Paper series, Sterling VA, December 2004, p. 5.
6. *OECD Observer*, May 2004, OECD, Brussels.
7. Extrapolated from M.C. Roco, *Government Nanotechnology Funding: An International Outlook*, 30 June 2003, table 1, www.nsf.gov.
8. *Select Committee on Science and Technology Fifth Report*, United Kingdom Parliament, Stationery Office, London, 2004, summary.
9. *Towards a European Strategy for Nanotechnology*, introduction.
10. Ibid., p. 8.
11. Jonathan Allum, 'Nanotechnology in Japan', *Japan Inc Magazine*, January 2003, www.japaninc.net.
12. Roco, *Government Nanotechnology Funding*.

13. *Select Committee on Science and Technology Fifth Report*, table 2 and para. 110.
14. 30 August 2004, www.investintaiwan.nat.gov.tw/en.
15. *OECD Observer*, May 2004.
16. *Jerusalem Post*, 6 March 2003.
17. *New York Times*, 21 December 2003.
18. *Chemical and Engineering News*, 1 September 2003.
19. *Select Committee on Science and Technology Fifth Report*, para. 23.
20. Ibid., para. 14.
21. *Chemical and Engineering News*, 1 September 2003.
22. 11 August 2004, www.smalltimes.com.
23. Testimony of Alan Marty of JP Morgan to Committee on Science, US House of Representatives, 19 March 2003.
24. Hope Shand, 'Gene Giants: Understanding the "Life Industry"', in Brian Tokar, ed., *Redesigning Life? The Worldwide Challenge to Genetic Engineering*, Zed Books, London, 2001, p. 225.
25. Ibid., p. 224.
26. Testimony of Alan Marty.
27. Cited in *Chemical and Engineering News*, 1 September 2003.
28. Testimony of Alan Marty.
29. 2 February 2005, www.smalltimes.com.
30. Company press release, 23 May 2002.
31. Steven Nottingham, *Eat Your Genes*, Zed Books, London, 2003, p. 111.
32. Ibid., p. 108.

Chapter 5

1. *Nanotechnology: What Is in Store for Us?*, Munich Re Group, Munich, 2002, p. 4.
2. Philip Anton, Richard Silberglitt and James Schneider, *The Global Technology Revolution*, RAND National Defense Research Institute, Santa Monica, 2001, p. xvii.
3. Doug Parr, Foreword, in Alexander Arnall, *Future Technologies, Today's Choices*, Greenpeace Environmental Trust, London, July 2003, p. 4.
4. *Nanotechnology: Small Matter, Many Unknowns*, Swiss Re, Zurich, 2004, p. 42.
5. Ibid., p. 43.
6. For an overview of the impact of nanoparticles on human health, see *Nanoscience and Nanotechnologies: Opportunities and Uncertainties*,

Royal Society and Royal Academy of Engineering, London, 2004, pp. 36–45.

7. *Nanotechnology: Small Matter, Many Unknowns*, p. 18.

8. *4th Nanoforum Report: Benefits, Risks, Ethical, Legal and Social Aspects of Nanotechnology*, www.nanoforum.org June 2004, p. 50.

9. Ibid., p. 46.

10. *Nanoscience and Nanotechnologies*, p. 71.

11. www.fda.gov/nanotechnology, link to FDA Regulation of Nanotechnology Products.

12. *Down on the Farm: The Impact of Nanoscale Technologies on Food and Agriculture*, ETC Group, Ottawa, November 2004, p. 53.

13. *Nanotechnology: What Is in Store for Us?*, p. 9.

14. *Down on the Farm*.

15. Jennifer Ferrara, 'Paving the Way for Biotechnology: Federal Regulations and Industry PR', in Brian Tokar, ed., *Redesigning Life: The Worldwide Challenge to Genetic Engineering*, Zed Books, London, 2001, pp. 297–303.

16. Stephen Nottingham, *Eat Your Genes*, Zed Books, London, 2003, p. 129.

17. Ibid., p. 132.

18. *Down on the Farm*, p. 39.

19. Interview with author, 27 January 2005.

20. *Nanotechnology: Small Matter, Many Unknowns*, p. 47.

21. *Nanotechnology: What Is in Store for Us?*, p. 11.

22. *4th Nanoforum Report*, p. 61.

23. Ibid., pp. 64–5.

24. 'Nanotechnology Pioneer Calms Fears of Runaway Replicators', www.foresight.org, 24 September 2004.

25. 'Living Robots Powered by Muscle', http://news.bbc.co.uk/2/hi/science/nature/4181197.stm.

26. China Economic Net, http://en-1.ce.cn/Life/environment/200412/11/t20041211_2552524.shtml.

27. Wei-xian Zhang, 'Nanoscale Iron Particles For Environmental Remediation: An Overview', *Journal of Nanoparticle Research* 5, 2003.

Chapter 6

1. Mark Avrum Gubrud, 'Nanotechnology and International Security', paper for the Fifth Foresight Conference on Molecular Nanotechnology, 2000, available at www.foresight.org/Conferences/MNT05/

Papers/Gubrud/.

2. *Nanotechnology: Its Impact on Defence and the MOD*, UK Ministry of Defence, London, 2001.

3. www.comw.org/qdr/qdr2001.pdf.

4. *Technology Trends: Preliminary Reports: Project on the Commercialisation of Space and the Development of Space Infrastructure: The Role of Public and Private Actors*, OECD General Secretariat, Brussels, May 2004, p. 15.

5. Manuel De Landa, *War in the Age of Intelligent Machines*, Zone Books, New York, 1991, p. 1.

6. *Nanotechnology and Risk*, Part 4, Center for Responsible Nanotechnology, November 2004, on www.crnana.org.

7. Paul Williams, *Osama's Revenge: The next 9/11*, Prometheus Books, New York, 2004, p. 153.

8. George Orwell, *Nineteen Eighty-four*, Penguin, London, 2000, p. 4.

Chapter 7

1. *Nanotechnology: Innovation for Tomorrow's World*, European Commission, Brussels, 2004, p. 28.

2. 'Human Development Report 2003 charts decade-long income drop in 54 countries', press release, UNDP, 8 July 2003, www.undp.org/hdr2003.

3. *World Energy Outlook 2002*, International Energy Agency, Paris, 2002, pp. 373–4.

4. Presentation in Washington DC, 17 June 2003.

5. See, for example, Sue Branford, 'Argentina's Bitter Harvest', *New Scientist*, 17 April 2004.

6. *Down on the Farm: The Impact of Nanoscale Technologies on Food and Agriculture*, ETC Group, Ottawa, November 2004, p. 8.

7. www.chinadaily.com, 7 October 2004.

8. Menzie Chinn and Robert Fairlie, *The Determinants of the Global Digital Divide: A Cross-country Analysis of Computer and Internet Penetration*, Yale University Economic Growth Center, discussion paper 881, March 2004, http://ssrn.com/abstract=519082, p. 7.

9. Philip Anton, Richard Silberglitt and James Schneider, *The Global Technology Revolution: Bio/nano/materials Trends and Their Synergies with Information Technology by 2015*, RAND National Defense Research Institute, Santa Monica CA, 2001, p. xvii.

10. 'Benefits, Risks, Ethical, Legal and Social Aspects of Nanotechnology',

Nanoforum.org, June 2004, available on www.nanoforum.org, pp. 88–9.
11. *Down on the Farm*, pp. 23–5.
12. 'Chemistry and Industry', Society of Chemical Engineers, London, 7 February 2005.
13. *Why Nanotechnology is So Important for the Semiconductor Industry*, NanoMarkets White Paper, NanoMarkets, Sterling VA, October 2004, p. 2.
14. *Austin Business Journal*, 13 September 2004.
15. 'Health Hazards in the Semiconductor Industry', *Asian Labour Update*, Hong Kong, July 2003.
16. Vivek Koppikar, Stephen Mabius and J. Steven Rurr, 'Current Trends in Nanotech Patents: A View from Inside the Patent Office', *Nanotechnology Law & Business*, vol. 1 no. 1, 2004, p. 2.
17. Ibid., p. 4.
18. *Nanotechnology – Size Matters: Building a Successful Nanotechnology Company*, 3i with the Economist Intelligence Unit and the Institute of Nanotechnology, London, July 2002, p. 17.
19. Ibid.
20. See, for example, the paper 'The True Cost of Gene Patents', Greenpeace, Hamburg, March 2004.

Chapter 8

1. *New Perspectives on Nanomemory*, NanoMarkets, Sterling VA, October 2004, p. 4.
2. Bill Joy, 'Why the Future Doesn't Need Us', *Wired*, April 2000.
3. *New York Times*, 16 February 2005.
4. See www.boycotttesco.com.
5. Rapporteur Alfred Nordmann, *Converging Technologies: Shaping the Future of European Societies*, European Commission, Brussels, 2004, p. 2.
6. Ibid., pp. 20–21 and pp. 32–4.
7. Ibid., p. 20.
8. Ibid., p. 21.

Chapter 9

1. www.smalltimes.com/document_display.cfm?document_id=8895.
2. *Nanotechnology and the Poor: Opportunities and Risks*, Meridian Institute,

Washington DC, January 2005, available at www.merid.org.

3. Ibid., p. 12.

4. *Wired*, April 2000.

5. *Nanotech News in Living Colour: An Update on White Papers, Red Flags, Green Goo, Grey Goo (and Red Herrings)*, ETC Group communiqué, ETC Group, Ottawa, Canada, May/June 2004.

6. Glenn Harlan Reynolds, *Forward to the Future: Nanotechnology and Regulatory Policy*, Pacific Research Institute, San Francisco CA, November 2002, p. 9.

7. Mike Treder, *Bridges to Safety and Bridges to Progress*, Center for Responsible Nanotechnology, November 2004, p. 6, www.crnano.org/Bridges.htm.

8. *People's Daily Online*, 2 March 2005, http://english.people.com.

9. Royal Society press release, 25 February 2005.

10. *Financial Times*, 26 February 2005.

11. *ESF Scientific Forward Look on Nanomedicine*, European Science Foundation, Strasbourg, February 2005, p. 3.

12. *India Daily*, 27 February 2005.

13. Yves Sandoz, 'ICRC involvement in banning or restricting the use of certain weapons', 9 February 2000, available on www.icrc.org.

14. For a discussion on capital and the impact of convergent technologies on the person, see Dany-Robert Dufour, 'De la réduction des têtes au changement des corps', *Le Monde Diplomatique*, April 2005.

15. www.sani.org.za/About.

16. *Nanotech News in Living Colour*.

17. Treder, *Bridges to Safety and Bridges to Progress*.

18. *Why International Development Might be Safest*, Center for Responsible Nanotechnology, www.crnano.org/development.htm.

Further reading

Many of the studies cited in the notes of this book are well-written and informative and worth reading in full. In so fast moving an area, though, those interested in keeping up with the subject will find it invaluable to sign up to some of the websites and email newsletters listed below:

- The *Institute of Nanotechnology* in Britain offers free associate membership along with higher, paying categories. Associate membership enables access to some reports and discussion groups. The Institute also publishes a newsletter. Its website is: www.nano.org.uk.
- The *Center for Responsible Nanotechnology* concentrates on nanotechnology as a manufacturing process, which it believes to be more imminent than do many others. The centre's website is www.crnano.org/ and it offers a number of papers and debates over the emerging technology. It lists thirty studies it has carried out on aspects of molecular manufacturing from timescales to dangers.
- The *ETC Group* (Action Group on Erosion, Technology and Concentration) has a wider brief than nanotechnology and this allows it to put the subject into a wider context. So it has produced interesting work on nanotechnology and agriculture, for example. The group's website is www.etcgroup.org/main.asp and

it is published in English, Spanish and French. The group is radical and critical of the direction nanotechnology is taking and advocates firm, international regulation.

- The *Foresight Institute* was established by nanotechnology guru Erik Drexler to educate the public about the emerging technology. In 2005 it revamped its mission statement, saying it would now be: 'refocusing our efforts on guiding nanotechnology research, public policy and education to address the critical challenges facing humanity. Foresight's new mission is to ensure the beneficial implementation of nanotechnology.' The institute organises conferences in the US but also carries papers, extracts, debates and news on www.foresight.org/.

- *Nanoforum* on www.nanoforum.org is a European Union sponsored source of information on nanotechnology. Publishing in several European languages, it offers access to papers on a wide variety of subjects from applications of nanotechnology in the space industry to assessments of social and ethical risks.

- For those wanting to keep up with the daily incremental advances made in laboratories around the world, http://science.physorg.com/ offers a free email newsletter with news releases from companies and universities.

- For an insight into the demands of the US nanotechnology business lobby, see www.nanobusiness.org/.

- *Nano Apec* is an industry research and media group, providing a series of electronic newsletters, found at www.nanoapex.com/.

- *Small Times* is a publisher of information on a range of technologies. Its site www.smalltimes.com/ provides industry news updates and access to online forums.

Index

About this series

'Communities in the South are facing great difficulties in coping with global trends. I hope this brave new series will throw much needed light on the issues ahead and help us choose the right options.'

MARTIN KHOR, *Director,*
Third World Network, Penang

'There is no more important campaign than our struggle to bring the global economy under democratic control. But the issues are fearsomely complex. This Global Issues series is a valuable resource for the committed campaigner and the educated citizen.'

BARRY COATES,
Director, Oxfam New Zealand

'Zed Books has long provided an inspiring list about the issues that touch and change people's lives. The Global Issues series is another dimension of Zed's fine record, allowing access to a range of subjects and authors that, to my knowledge, very few publishers have tried. I strongly recommend these new, powerful titles and this exciting series.'

JOHN PILGER, *author*

'We are all part of a generation that actually has the means to eliminate extreme poverty world-wide. Our task is to harness the forces of globalization for the benefit of working people, their families and their communities – that is our collective duty. The Global Issues series makes a powerful contribution to the global campaign for justice, sustainable and equitable development, and peaceful progress.'

GLENYS KINNOCK, *MEP*

The Global Issues series

Already available

Peggy Antrobus, *The Global Women's Movement: Origins, Issues and Strategies*

Walden Bello, *Deglobalization: Ideas for a New World Economy*

Robert Ali Brac de la Perrière and Franck Seuret, *Brave New Seeds: The Threat of GM Crops to Farmers*

Greg Buckman, *Globalization: Tame it or Scrap It?*

Greg Buckman, *Global Trade: Past Mistakes, Future Choices*

Ha-Joon Chang and Ilene Grabel, *Reclaiming Development: An Alternative Economic Policy Manual*

Koen De Feyter, *Human Rights: Social Justice in the Age of the Market*

Oswaldo de Rivero, *The Myth of Development: The Non-viable Economies of the 21st Century*

Graham Dunkley, *Free Trade: Myth, Reality and Alternatives*

Joyeeta Gupta, *Our Simmering Planet: What to Do about Global Warming?*

Nicholas Guyatt, *Another American Century? The United States and the World since 9/11*

Ann-Christin Sjölander Holland, *Water for Sale? Corporations against People*

Martin Khor, *Rethinking Globalization: Critical Issues and Policy Choices*

John Madeley, *Food for All: The Need for a New Agriculture*

John Madeley, *Hungry for Trade: How the Poor Pay for Free Trade*

Damien Millet and Eric Toussaint, *Who Owes Who? 50 Questions About World Debt*

Paola Monzini, *Sex Traffic: Prostitution, Crime and Exploitation*

Jonathon W. Moses, *International Migration: Globalization's Last Frontier*

A.G. Noorani, *Islam and Jihad: Prejudice versus Reality*

Riccardo Petrella, *The Water Manifesto: Arguments for a World Water Contract*

Peter Robbins, *Stolen Fruit: The Tropical Commodities Disaster*

Toby Shelley, *Oil: Politics, Poverty and the Planet*

Toby Shelley, *Nanotechnology: New Promises, New Dangers*

Vandana Shiva, *Protect or Plunder? Understanding Intellectual Property Rights*

Harry Shutt, *A New Democracy: Alternatives to a Bankrupt World Order*

David Sogge, *Give and Take: What's the Matter with Foreign Aid?*

Vivien Stern, *Creating Criminals: Prisons and People in a Market Society*

Paul Todd and Jonathan Bloch, *Global Intelligence: The World's Secret Services Today*

In preparation

Liz Kelly, *Violence against Women*

Alan Marshall, *A New Nuclear Age? The Case for Nuclear Power Revisited*

Roger Moody, *Digging the Dirt: The Modern World of Global Mining*

Edgar Pieterse, *City Futures: Confronting the Crisis of Urban Development*

Peter M. Rosset, *Food is Not Just Another Commodity: Why the WTO Should Get Out of Agriculture*

For full details of this list and Zed's other subject and general catalogues, please write to: The Marketing Department, Zed Books, 7 Cynthia Street, London N1 9JF, UK or email Sales@zedbooks.net

Visit our website at: www.zedbooks.co.uk

Participating organizations

Both ENDS A service and advocacy organization which collaborates with environment and indigenous organizations, both in the South and in the North, with the aim of helping to create and sustain a vigilant and effective environmental movement.

Nieuwe Keizersgracht 45, 1018 VC Amsterdam, The Netherlands
Phone: +31 20 623 0823   Fax: +31 20 620 8049
Email: info@bothends.org   Website: www.bothends.org

Catholic Institute for International Relations (CIIR) CIIR aims to contribute to the eradication of poverty through a programme that combines advocacy at national and international level with community-based development.

Unit 3, Canonbury Yard, 190a New North Road, London N1 7BJ, UK
Phone +44 (0)20 7354 0883   Fax +44 (0)20 7359 0017
Email: ciir@ciir.org   Website: www.ciir.org

Corner House The Corner House is a UK-based research and solidarity group working on social and environmental justice issues in North and South.

PO Box 3137, Station Road, Sturminster Newton, Dorset DT10 1YJ, UK
Tel.: +44 (0)1258 473795   Fax: +44 (0)1258 473748
Email: cornerhouse@gn.apc.org Website: www.cornerhouse.icaap.org

Council on International and Public Affairs (CIPA) CIPA is a human rights research, education and advocacy group, with a particular focus on economic and social rights in the USA and elsewhere around the world. Emphasis in recent years has been given to resistance to corporate domination.

777 United Nations Plaza, Suite 3C, New York, NY 10017, USA
Tel. +1 212 972 9877   Fax +1 212 972 9878
Email: cipany@igc.org   Website: www.cipa-apex.org

Dag Hammarskjöld Foundation The Dag Hammarskjöld Foundation, established 1962, organises seminars and workshops on social, economic and cultural issues facing developing countries with a particular focus on alternative and innovative solutions. Results are published in its journal *Develpment Dialogue*.

Övre Slottsgatan 2, 753 10 Uppsala, Sweden.
Tel.: +46 18 102772   Fax: +46 18 122072
Email: secretariat@dhf.uu.se   Website: www.dhf.uu.se

Development GAP The Development Group for Alternative Policies is a Non-Profit Development Resource Organization working with popular organizations in the South and their Northern partners in support of a development that is truly sustainable and that advances social justice.

927 15th Street NW, 4th Floor, Washington, DC, 20005, USA
Tel.: +1 202 898 1566   Fax: +1 202 898 1612
E-mail: dgap@igc.org   Website: www.developmentgap.org

Focus on the Global South Focus is dedicated to regional and global policy analysis and advocacy work. It works to strengthen the capacity of organizations of the poor and marginalized people of the South and to better analyse and understand the impacts of the globalization process on their daily lives.

C/o CUSRI, Chulalongkorn University, Bangkok 10330, Thailand
Tel.: +66 2 218 7363 Fax: +66 2 255 9976
Email: Admin@focusweb.org   Website: www.focusweb.org

IBON IBON Foundation is a research, education and information institution that provides publications and services on socio-economic issues as support to advocacy in the Philippines and abroad. Through its research and databank, formal and non-formal education programmes, media work and international networking, IBON aims to build the capacity of both Philippine and international organizations.

Room 303 SCC Bldg, 4427 Int. Old Sta. Mesa, Manila 1008, Philippines
Phone +632 7132729   Fax +632 7160108
Email: editors@ibon.org   Website: www.ibon.org

Inter Pares Inter Pares, a Canadian social justice organization, has been active since 1975 in building relationships with Third World development groups and providing support for community-based development programmes. Inter Pares is also involved in education and advocacy in Canada, promoting understanding about the causes, effects and solutions to poverty.

221 Laurier Avenue East, Ottawa, Ontario, KIN 6PI Canada
Phone +1 613 563 4801   Fax +1 613 594 4704
Email: info@interpares.ca   Website: www.interpares.ca

Public Interest Research Centre PIRC is a research and campaigning group based in Delhi which seeks to serve the information needs of activists and organizations working on macro-economic issues concerning finance, trade and development.

142 Maitri Apartments, Plot No. 28, Patparganj, Delhi 110092, India
Phone: +91 11 2221081/2432054   Fax: +91 11 2224233
Email: kaval@nde.vsnl.net.in

Third World Network   TWN is an international network of groups and individuals involved in efforts to bring about a greater articulation of the needs and rights of peoples in the Third World; a fair distribution of the world's resources; and forms of development which are ecologically sustainable and fulfil human needs. Its international secretariat is based in Penang, Malaysia.

121-S Jalan Utama, 10450 Penang, Malaysia
Tel.: +60 4 226 6159   Fax: +60 4 226 4505
Email: twnet@po.jaring.my   Website: www.twnside.org.sg

Third World Network–Africa   TWN–Africa is engaged in research and advocacy on economic, environmental and gender issues. In relation to its current particular interest in globalization and Africa, its work focuses on trade and investment, the extractive sectors and gender and economic reform.

2 Ollenu Street, East Legon, PO Box AN19452, Accra-North, Ghana.
Tel.: +233 21 511189/503669/500419   Fax: +233 21 511188
Email: twnafrica@ghana.com

World Development Movement (WDM)   The World Development Movement campaigns to tackle the causes of poverty and injustice. It is a democratic membership movement that works with partners in the South to cancel unpayable debt and break the ties of IMF conditionality, for fairer trade and investment rules, and for strong international rules on multinationals.

25 Beehive Place, London SW9 7QR, UK
Tel.: +44 (0)20 7737 6215   Fax: +44 (0)20 7274 8232
Email: wdm@wdm.org.uk   Website: www.wdm.org.uk

This book is also available in the following countries

CARIBBEAN

Arawak Publications
17 Kensington Crescent
Apt 5
Kingston 5, Jamaica
Tel: 876 960 7538
Fax: 876 960 9219

EGYPT

MERIC
2 Bahgat Ali Street,
Tower D/Apt. 24
Zamalek, Cairo
Tel: 20 2 735 3818/3824
Fax: 20 2 736 9355

FIJI

University Book Centre,
University of South Pacific
Suva
Tel: 679 313 900
Fax: 679 303 265

GUYANA

Austin's Book Services
190 Church St
Cummingsburg
Georgetown
austins@guyana.net.gy
Tel: 592 227 7395
Fax: 592 227 7396

IRAN

Book City
743 North Hafez Avenue
15977 Tehran
Tel: 98 21 889 7875
Fax: 98 21 889 7785
bookcity@neda.net

MAURITIUS

Editions Le Printemps
4 Club Rd, Vacoas

NAMIBIA

Book Den
PO Box 3469, Shop 4
Frans Indongo Gardens
Windhoek
Tel: 264 61 239976
Fax: 264 61 234248

NEPAL

Everest Media Services,
GPO Box 5443
Dillibazar
Putalisadak Chowk
Kathmandu
Tel: 977 1 416026
Fax: 977 1 250176

NIGERIA

Mosuro Publishers
52 Magazine Road
Jericho, Ibadan
Tel: 234 2 241 3375
Fax: 234 2 241 3374

PAKISTAN

Vanguard Books
45 The Mall, Lahore
Tel: 92 42 735 5079
Fax: 92 42 735 5197

PAPUA NEW GUINEA

Unisearch PNG Pty Ltd
Box 320, University
National Capital District
Tel: 675 326 0130
Fax: 675 326 0127

RWANDA

Librairie Ikirezi
PO Box 443, Kigali
Tel/Fax: 250 71314

SUDAN

The Nile Bookshop
New Extension Street 41
PO Box 8036, Khartoum
Tel: 249 11 463 749

UGANDA

Aristoc Booklex Ltd
PO Box 5130, Kampala Rd
Diamond Trust Building
Kampala
Tel/Fax: 256 41 254867

ZAMBIA

UNZA Press
PO Box 32379, Lusaka
Tel: 260 1 290409
Fax: 260 1 253952